God invites all people from all walks of life throughout all time to join His eternal loving holy family through Jesus' sacrificial death on a wooden cross (John 3:16; Heb 10:12).

Victory In Jesus
Being a Child of God
Fourth Edition

by Dr. James B. Joseph
"Brother James"

IJSP

In Jesus' Service Publishing
Pfafftown, NC

First Edition published in 1997

Fourth Edition 2025
English-Paperback ISBN: 979-8-9905963-6-8
Library of Congress Control Number: 2024926690

In Jesus' Service Publishing (IJSP)
www.injesusservice.com

**"Your Word is a lamp to my feet,
indeed, a light to my pathway!"
Psalm 119:105**

**Through the guidance
of the Father
and help of the Holy Spirit,
let's follow Jesus faithfully!**

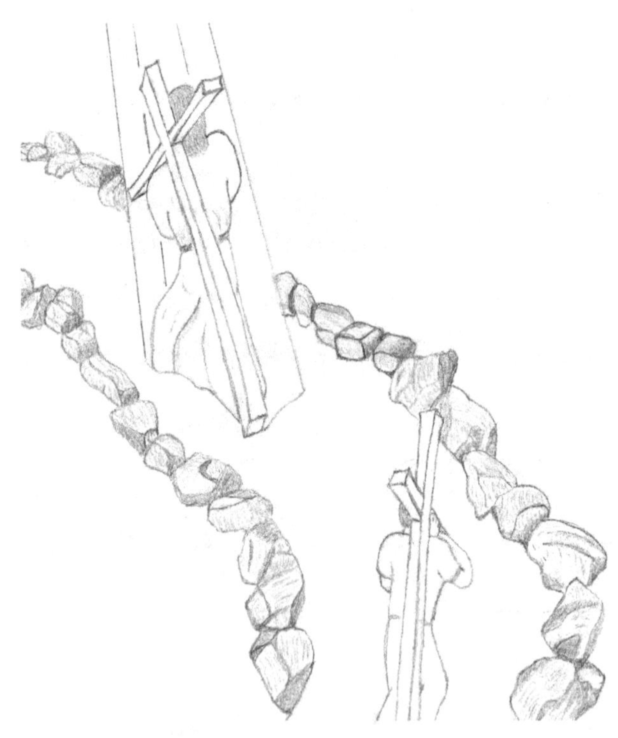

Dedication

Victory In Jesus. . . Being a Child of God **is dedicated to God's Kingdom Work on Earth. It is dedicated to the Father, the Son, the Spirit of Truth, and to all who are striving to walk in our Father's will. Let us strongly resist being conformed to the ways of this world, and let us allow God to transform us into His loving righteous children proving His good and acceptable way of life. As we journey through this side of eternity, let us lead many to God showing His goodness through our actions and words as we overcome Satan's many deceptions through God's enlightenment and power.**

Statements by Various Denominational Church Leaders Who Read the First Edition of **VICTORY IN JESUS: Being a Child of God**

"One may well take a giant step in spiritual understanding and growth by reading/studying *Victory In Jesus*. The insights set forth in James Joseph's book are worthy of one's time and mental energy,"

Dr. Cecil R. Cave, Jr. – Pastor,
Mineral Springs Baptist Church

"I have every confidence that people who will read and follow *Victory In Jesus* will turn a corner in their life. That turning will lead them on a successful journey toward living a victorious life in Christ,"

Dr. James C. Hash – Senior Pastor,
St. Peter's World Outreach Center

"Through his careful study of the Scriptures, James Joseph has produced a book that can be helpful for people who are seeking to know God's will for living in unity with God and neighbor,"

Rev. Robert S. Roller – Pastor,
Fraternity Church of the Brethren

"You will be stimulated and blessed by the reading of this book. It is a fresh call for practical unity in the Body. Here is a work that proclaims great biblical truths on unity and provides practical helps for churches and individuals on working together for the cause of Christ,"

Dr. Mark Corts – Senior Pastor,
Calvary Baptist Church

Statements by Various Denominational Church Leaders Who Read the First Edition (cont.)

"In this book, James gives a dynamic challenge to every Christian to sojourn and carry out the Great Commission. . . . In addition, this book lays out in practical terms the needed insight and motivation for every Christian leader in the twenty-first century,"

Rev. Larry A. Boyd – Pastor,
New Covenant Non-denominational Church

"*Victory In Jesus: Being a Child of God* offers great insight into the nature of the Church. You will find this work very useful as a Bible study guide especially for community groups seeking guidance as they plan interdenominational ministries,"

Rev. G. Thomas Shelton – Pastor,
Friedburg Moravian Church

"Here is a book that challenges us, from a biblical and theological perspective, to be the united Body of Christ showing our communities the reality of the risen Christ,"

Dr. Bob Neff – Pastor,
Cornerstone Community Church

"I am touched by the sincerity and convictions with which James Joseph expressed his faith in his book *Victory In Jesus*. His work helps us understand how the Gospel is, at once, simple and yet utterly profound. My prayer is that it will be a blessing to those who read it,"

Dr. George P. Robinson – Senior Minister,
Centenary United Methodist Church

Foreword

VICTORY IN JESUS and my other books have been written to help those who want to understand more fully their God-given purpose in life and wish to experience more godly joy as they follow Jesus. Christ prayed that His followers would experience His joy, which was made full at the Cross because He was providing eternal perfection within the Family of God for those who learned to listen to Him.

The Bible is clear that God invites every person of every generation to join Him in becoming a member of His eternal close-knit holy family. Upon receiving God into one's life, every member is asked to help others who are still living separate from God to know Him and join His eternal family and kingdom. Through the Holy Spirit, God develops love *for all* in the hearts of His family members and commissions each of them to be His representatives on earth. Like Christ, His followers experience great joy over every individual who is rescued from the deceptions of self-centeredness, selfishness, and Satan.

As you realize more fully what God is asking of you and what Satan is doing to quench the leading of the Holy Spirit, you will be liberated to follow Christ more fully into spiritual battle resulting in more coming to know God and desiring to be part of His eternal family. Through God's children becoming more interactive within His Creation, God will become more fully known and trusted worldwide.

VICTORY IN JESUS: Being a Child of God addresses real and serious issues such as the fact that God wants everyone to join His family and the fact that every follower of Jesus belongs first to the Universal Church and then their local congregations. This book also helps followers of Jesus understand their place in God's Family more fully so that they may truly experience more of Jesus' joy as they help one another and bring others into His family and kingdom.

Foreword (cont.)

This brief book encourages all of Christ's followers to pursue a proper interactive relationship with God under Jesus' lordship. The readers come to realize more fully that God's love and superiority overcome current trials and tribulations and helps to reveal the deceptions of Satan. It helps shed light on many areas of our lives that flourish with God's leadership and addresses critical spiritual issues shedding light on our ongoing spiritual battles between good and evil.

Over the years, I have seen many Christians who are not very excited about their walk with God. I have come to realize that *Satan has deceived many into thinking that they have been saved through some type of a pass to heaven instead of a genuine relationship with God.* This book will help its readers understand more fully God's desire for everyone to join His eternal close holy family and what that looks like as we live out our lives following Jesus. Following Jesus should produce great joy and inner peace even as His followers go through ongoing spiritual battles.

An exciting eternally rewarding life starts with a genuine commitment to follow Jesus. *God does not accept lukewarm followers.* While under great duress, just prior to going to the Cross for all people of all time, Jesus prayed that those who followed Him would experience the same joy that He was experiencing as He looked at the great salvation made possible for all who learned to love, trust, and obey God (John 17:13). Jesus said that His followers would do greater works than He had done up to the point of His sacrificial death (John 14:12) referring to their future labors when they would join Him in bringing many into God's Kingdom and family through the empowerment of the Holy Spirit. God, the Father, wants Jesus' follower to overcome the deceptions of Satan and lead many into His glorious eternal presence.

It is my prayer that the biblical truths within this book will encourage and energize you to study and apply abundantly God's Word, the Bible, to your life. As your understanding of your place in God's family grows, you will find yourself more available to do

Foreword (cont.)

those things that are pleasing to Him. Enjoy obtaining something more precious than gold as you study the scriptural truths that lie within this little book.

If you wish to study further, consider reading *Experiencing Jesus' Joy* and *The Ultimate Victory: Becoming a Follower of Jesus.* They are available from Amazon, many retailers, and through the author's website:

www.injesusservice.com

May we follow Jesus into the good works that God has assigned to each of us prior to putting the physical universe into motion (Eph 2:10)!

Table of Contents

Table of Contents (cont.)

Introduction
Transformation Brings Inner Peace

Be not conformed to this Age, but be transformed by the renewal of your mind proving what is the good, acceptable, and complete will of God. Romans 12:2[1]

All of us have felt God touch and stir our innermost thoughts at various times as He encouraged us to slow down and think about our very existence and His will for our lives. He has awakened some of us in the middle of the night, arrested our thoughts on the way to work, or heightened our senses as we quietly read His Word. During these precious spiritual awakening moments, He has encouraged us to look beyond ourselves and the immediate future to consider all existence, eternity, and how we individually are to fit into the total scheme of things.

Most of us feel uncomfortable during these special times because God encourages us to face the reality of His desire for our lives. He tells us on an ongoing basis that He loves us and desires to mold us into caring individuals who will join Him as He ministers to all. During these special times of stirring, He forces us to look beyond the immediate and consider the long range consequences of our actions encouraging us to learn to trust and follow Him so that He can transform us into His loving and morally righteous children.

Where we are today in our relationship with God is not as important as where we will be tomorrow. Wherever we are, He

---

[1] For all New Testament Scripture quotations within this work, I have translated Greek text from the United Bible Societies' 3rd ed. (Nestle 26) into English.

continually shapes us desiring that we ultimately will be able to live with Him in perfect godly unity based on godly love.

When you allow God to speak to your heart, He draws you close and encourages you to join Him in His creative work of love as He ministers to all drawing as many as will listen into His eternal close-knit holy family. But, if you allow your own selfishness, exaggerated self-worth (pride), or someone else other than God to guide your life, an emptiness may overshadow you that cannot be filled through any type of general busyness, good works, or entertainment. Although staying busy may temporarily drown out God's voice and block His message of love, it is no substitute for a meaningful relationship with Him, which brings true inner peace coupled with a growing trust in Him.

As we carry out the will of God, He places inner peace in our hearts through Jesus Christ. Jesus, the Savior of the World, came into our world at His appointed time to provide all humanity forgiveness, purification, and reconciliation through His death on a cross, and Jesus' followers are those who hear and accept this message of love and purification.

When we turn from our own ways to our Heavenly Father and His ways receiving Him into our lives as our leader, He immediately starts transforming us into the likeness of His Son, Jesus, replacing our emptiness, shame, and fear with love, joy, and inner peace. This peace comes only through making peace with the One who created us for a caring fellowship full of good woks. Through submission to God's will, God's love and resulting hierarchy of order enables us to live in peace and harmony with Him and all others who have submitted to His lordship.

Submitting to the Creator's authority is difficult at first because we have to learn to put our own interests on an equal footing with all others and allow God to direct us. With God's help, we can be developed beyond our initial child-like selfish nature. Although we are born into this world with a child-like nature that many times wants immediate satisfaction and disregards the cost of our actions to others, God has a perfect plan of development for each of us.

If we allow God to develop us to be more like Jesus, we will not live out our physical lives as if there were no future and end up separated from God for eternity. We will learn to listen to our Heavenly Father through Jesus' leadership through the Holy Spirit and trust and obey God because of His great ongoing unbiased love for all. If we truly want everlasting peace and harmony, we will learn to accept God's will above our own knowing that His ways will bring good to us and all who listen. When we make a conscious effort to submit to our Heavenly Father and turn from our way of life to His, which is called "repentance," we immediately obtain ***victory*** over this world and death. Upon genuine repentance, submission, and commitment, God has promised that He will conform our nature into the image of His Son Jesus, the Prophesied Messiah (Christ), free from sin.

Godly Fellowship

When speaking of solitary individuals, "one" is a lonely number that in reality applies to God as well as humanity. In spite of the many forms of life created at the beginning of the Creation, God said that it was not good for Adam to be without a suitable help mate, and therefore, He created Eve whom Adam could relate to as a partner and share his life.

Similarly, we see our Heavenly Father working with His beloved Son, Jesus, creating a people who could provide suitable companionship for Him. A people whom the Father, Son, and Holy Spirit could relate to and share their lives; a people who could join Them in their good works. They are asking all people to join them in a mature eternal free-will interactive relationship that provides great joy and peace; this relationship is based on godly unity, a "one/oneness," that brings great joy and inner peace.

During our time on Earth, God normally interacts with all people mostly unseen and yet closely as a loving parent. He watches over His children carefully. Yet, He cannot fully share His life with us on a mature level until we are perfected, which includes removal of all of our bad actions (sin). Similarly as adults, we cannot live on the same level of intimacy with our young children as we can with some of our adult children and mature close friends.

To make a close, mature, and eternal relationship possible, our Heavenly Father is at work in a special way developing those who listen. He develops us daily encouraging us to join Him in His good works, and He waits for the time that He will bring us Home to be in Heaven with Him for eternity. In a similar manner, we work with our children as they are developing waiting for the day that we may obtain a closer mature relationship with them as adults.

There is one major difference between God's development for us and our development for our children. God promises all who accept His love through submission of their will to His that He will ***totally transform*** their nature to be like Jesus' yet keeping each's individualism intact.

Abundant free will plays a strong role in God's desire for fellowship with us. Although God strongly encourages all people to learn to live with Him and each other in godly fellowship, He does not force anyone to do so. God gives all people the ability to accept or reject His love and authority.

But, beware, abundant free will does not give us a license to do whatever we want without eventually paying tremendous consequences for our actions against God and man. If we do not allow God to develop us into good social beings, He separates us from Himself and His obedient children for eternity. If we do not listen to God, which includes joining Him in His Great Work of Love, ***which is the Realization of His Creation through the Cross with its New Heaven and Earth and perfected family,*** we will not have eternal fellowship with Him within His eternal holy family.

Abundant free will is essential in God's plan for an equal, mature, and multi-person relationship with all who listen. Give-and-take relationships based upon ***equality of being*** require free will. Until we learn to truly love God and each other as Jesus loves us, our self-centeredness and pride will continue to hurt others producing heart-felt pain for all. We should strive to love one another with the same love and compassion that the Father, Jesus, and the Holy Spirit have for us. Their incredible love for us compelled Jesus to follow our Heavenly Father's will and die on a cross making a way for all to live with them in sinless peace and harmony forever.

Jesus has demonstrated His love for us and commands us to love our neighbors as He loves us. Now, we must allow God to teach us to love as He loves; our love for one another should be based on God's love for us not on how we feel.

Although there is much pain associated with our earthly stages of development, there is a much greater joy associated with our godly transformation as our nature becomes more and more like Jesus'. As part of the Creation, God has given all of us some of His own personal qualities that can be developed if we listen to Him. As we submit to His will, He develops our nature to include more and more grace and truthfulness.

None of us walk perfectly with God, yet we have peace knowing that God is not looking so much at the present, but instead He is looking down the road into eternity. As God put the Creation into motion, He looked into the future and said that His Creation with its abundant free will, which resulted in a fair amount of sin and resulting tribulation, would in the long run end up with an ultimate victory for all who learned to live with Him according to His holy ways. And considering the final outcome, He said that His Creation was "good-exceedingly."

Knowing that all of us would go through some stages of rebellion, our Heavenly Father has provided ***all*** people a path, a journey through life, that leads to maturity, perfection, and peace if we listen to Him. This one and only path leading to eternal joy and inner peace starts by obediently following His son, Jesus. Keep in mind that Jesus is the one who created physically, the entire Universe.

God knew before He physically created our world that all would initially go through times of disobedience as we developed. Therefore, prior to implementing the physical Creation, the Father made plans to send Jesus to the Cross to atone for our disobedience and to cleanse/remove our bad actions if we would learn to return His love and desire His way of life.

He gave Jesus the responsibility of saving us and guiding us home to be with Them forever. As we follow Jesus, our Heavenly Father continually offers us a fresh start through repentance, which includes turning from our way of life to His and asking for forgiveness of our wrongdoings. Therefore, we must stop being a slave to our past sins. God encourages us to pray for forgiveness of our sins and make atonement for them and forget them as we strive to walk in His ways proclaiming His goodness to those who will listen.

We cannot learn to have this full-time relationship with our Heavenly Father exclusively through head knowledge, our parents, friends, or positions within our local churches. Although many of us attend a local church regularly and contribute something to God's work through the giving of our time and resources, God is asking everyone to join Him in something much more fulfilling than being a spectator or lukewarm part-time follower of Jesus. God is asking all of us to join Him in a ***full-time*** interactive personal relationship that is so powerful that it will transform the very nature of our lives and those around us for eternity. But take note, we must ***each*** decide to accept or reject His full-time eternal interactive plan for our lives.

Joining God in His Work

Beware, Satan is at work in our busy world trying to destroy as many lives as possible. There are many people who are being distracted by him, and therefore, they are not listening to God. Many of the distractions are temporarily pleasing to us. Individuals who are being distracted by Satan can keep us so preoccupied through work or entertainment that we do not take any real time to listen to the Creator. In addition, when we decide to listen for a few moments and then discuss God with fellow followers of Jesus, we may come away discouraged because some, who claim to follow Jesus, do not know God personally; they only know ***about*** Him. If we ask and follow their advice as we seek to follow God's will, we will hear many mixed messages.

When our Father speaks to you, do not let Satan come and steal away the gold that God gives you. Read His written Word, the Bible, on a regular basis and let Him speak to your heart confirming in you that He is real, awesome, loves you, and wants to guide your life. Jesus continually listens to the Father and guides all who listen with Him on a path to eternal joy and peace, and He strongly warns all of us about going off and doing ministry under our own power instead of being directed and empowered by Him.

This book will supply you with the conceptual tools needed to understand God, His Creation, and your place within His Creation more fully as you study key scriptures within the Bible. You are very precious to God and He has good things stored up for you to do. As we listen to God, He teaches us to work together in godly unity with Him in our communities and around the world proclaiming His grace through our actions as well as our words.

Note: Before proceeding, let's look at the basic relationship between several individuals and how they will be declared throughout this book: God, Creator, Father, and Heavenly Father; Son, Jesus, Jesus Christ, Messiah, the Anointed One, and Eldest Brother; and Holy Spirit, the Spirit of Truth. Scripturally, the term "God" refers normally to all three, the "Father," "Son," and "Holy Spirit," working together in perfect "oneness" (Tri-unity/Trinity) ***or*** solely to the Father because of His supreme authority and power over all including Jesus, the Messiah, and the Holy Spirit. Although the Father, Son, and Holy Spirit work together in perfect unity under the eternal leadership of the Father, there are many circumstances in which one of them has a predominate role in some action. Their predominate roles are normally emphasized by specifically referring to the appropriate individual for that particular circumstance remembering that they are always working ***together*** in perfect godly unity. In no circumstance, can you leave one of them out of the picture and see it clearly.

Chapter 1
Understanding Eternal Life

If you remain in my word, you are truly my disciples, and you shall know the truth (reality), and the truth shall set you free. John 8:31-32

If we continue to take time to study and act on God's Word, Jesus will teach us to know and act on truth/reality so that we may be freed from our individual desires to sin. Our desire to sin is caused primarily by our selfishness, lack of godly knowledge, and direct disobedience and rebellion against God.[2] Our Heavenly Father has appointed Jesus Christ to free all who listen so that we may eventually live together in perfect fellowship with no more sorrows.[3] As we read on a regular basis and obediently act on God's Word, we learn God's ways more fully and are more open to His leading as He guides us during our life on Earth. Our Heavenly Father promises all who listen that He will work with us and complete our perfection including complete sin removal.[4] Our nature will eventually be totally transformed to be like Jesus'.[5]

After God created the universe and our immediate world according to types, They created us ***in Their own image*** according to ***Their own likeness*** for eternal fellowship.[6] God wants a mature

---

[2] John 18:37; 2 Tim 4:3-4; 1 Peter 1:13-14; 2 Peter 1:4; Jude 14-18.

[3] Rev 21:3-4.

[4] Gal 3:13-14; Col 2:13-14; 2 Cor 5:21; 1 Peter 2:24; cf. Isa 53:5.

[5] Phil 1:6; Rom 8:28-30; 1 John 3:1-3.

[6] Gen 1:26-27.

intimate relationship with us, and although They have created everyone for eternal fellowship and good works with Them, They do not force anyone to join Them. Over time, They teach and perfect all who learn to trust and obey Them because of Their great love for all.

Because of our initial immaturity, our Heavenly Father deliberately starts our eternal life with a physically and spiritually limited capacity to slow us down and give us a chance to consider and choose between an eternal life of ***good***, which is based on learning to love through submission to His will, or ***evil***, which is based on maintaining a self-centered selfish life through ongoing disobedience to Him and His way of life. God's love is based on impartial love for ***all***.

Our limited physical capacity stops us from destroying ourselves and everyone around us immediately although there is plenty of destruction and hurt in the creation process. You wouldn't give a three year old a five-thousand pound automobile to drive, would you? If we allow God to mature us, we are given much greater ability and corresponding power after our physical death,[7] and through God's righteous assigned good works for each of us, we will help many people along our individual life journeys.

The Creation Is Moving toward Its Final Form

Keep in mind that this is God's creation! He knows what He is doing, and He is totally capable of completing it perfectly! After the start of His Creation, God considered what He had done and where it was headed according to His plans, and He said that it was "good exceedingly [Gen 1:31]." Prior to physically starting the Creation, God knew how each person throughout the entire Creation would respond to His love and lordship (foreknowledge).[8]

---

[7] Rom 8:16-18; 1 John 3:1-3; Rev 3:20-21.

[8] Eph 1:3-8; 1 Peter 1:1-2; Rom 8:28-30.

When we consider God's end goal, His perfected family living in the sinless New Heaven and New Earth, we realize that His creation is not over until He fills up His Family. At that time, He will eternally separate His completed holy eternal volunteer family from all who did not learn to love, trust, and obey Him throughout the entire Creation.

So, how active is God during the creation process? With so much evil going on due to abundant free will, some question God's day-to-day involvement in His own Creation. Let's consider the fact that even though God asks all humanity to take care of one another and life in general, it is God– not us –who has been doing the heavy lifting throughout the entire creative process. Although God is sovereign, He is also a serving sustainer (Matt 20:28; Mark 10:45) asking everyone to learn to serve one another. Keep in mind that the Sent Son of God, Jesus, was born in a manger but could have been born in a palace if the Father so desired, and that He grew up doing manual labor as a carpenter's son instead of growing up as an earthly prince or king.

Not being limited by time, God knew in advance what it would take to create a mature free-will intimate loving righteous (holy) family. He also knew ahead of time who throughout the Creation would want to become part of His eternal loving family receiving Him as lord as well as savior. These are the "called" and "chosen" of God.[9] The Father also knew in advance that it was "necessary"[10] to send His Son, Jesus, to die for all humanity in order to bring those who would learn to love Him into a final eternal sinless resurrected state.

So, prior to starting the physical Creation, the Father, Son, and Holy Spirit planned out a death within the Trinity. They would suffer tremendously as the Son died a physical death and was also separated from the Father (spiritual death) personally taking on the

---

[9] Matt 25:34; Rom 8:28; Eph 1:3-5; 1 Peter 1:1-5.

[10] Greek *dei*; see John 3:14-15.

bad actions of all people over the entire Creation[11] who learned to trust Them. For those who would learn to trust and obey Them out of a developing love for all, Jesus would remove their sin taking each's bad actions onto Himself in order to eliminate it forever after spending His three days in Sheol/Hades.[12]

Although we cannot remove bad actions (sin) from one another, if we could, it might be comparable to someone being able to remove all cancerous cells from someone else by personally absorbing these bad cells into himself and replacing them with his own healthy cells and in the end dying due to the cancer now ravaging his own body.

God makes sure that no matter what circumstance one is born into, everyone will understand that He desires ***all*** to be part of His family and live holy lives. Although everyone is born into sin under the many deceptions of Satan, all have a chance to overcome evil as God teaches ***everyone*** the reality of His Creation and His requirements for eternal life, which eventually brings some to the point of wanting to do His will and follow His holy ways.

God Wants To Be Your Friend

In the perfected eternal world that God is creating, there has to be pure righteous leadership in order to keep the family cohesively living together without sin. Therefore, during our physical life, ***individuals must decide if God is worthy of their love, respect, and obedience***. In this process, God takes the lead and helps everyone know Him and His righteous way of life asking everyone to learn to love, trust, and obey Him.[13] Jesus is the perfect example of the loving, trusting, and obedient Son doing those

---

[11] Heb 10:10-14.

[12] Acts 2:22-33; Heb 1:2-3; cf. Gal 3:13-14; 1 Peter 2:24; 2 Cor 5:21; Col 2:13-14; Rev 21:3-4.

[13] John 14:15, 21, 23; 15:10; cf. Rom 1:18-2:16.

things that please His Heavenly Father at all times.[14] In addition, Jesus told His present and future obedient disciples that not only were they family members, but that they were also His friends and that there is no greater love than someone being willing to die for his friends (John 15:13-14).Within God's family, all members are friends with one another. When Peter was challenged by Jesus to help guide the Church, He asked Peter three times if he really loved Him. Peter responded each time by telling Jesus that he loved Him as a good friend, which is the closest kind of relational love.[15]

Getting Off the Wide-Road That Leads to Destruction

Knowing that God wants everyone to learn to return His love, why do so many stay on the wide-road (life-path) that leads to a lower quality life now and an eventual permanent separation from God instead of receiving God into their lives? With God doing so much to help everyone have a better life, it would seem that most people would get off the wide-road leading to destruction and follow God's path for their lives. But in reality, an elevated sense of self-worth (pride) along with Satan's regular encouragement to rebel against God keeps many content to follow their own desires instead of God's.

With the many distractions of present life, if we ignore God speaking to our hearts (God's self-revelation/spiritual awakening), we will fail to know and love Him for who He is. He is a loving caring creator and father. Our primary obligation is to learn to return His love while He constantly works with us; He is worthy of our love, trust, and obedience.[16]

In addition, if we want to be with God, we must allow Him to break through our personal activities and Satan's deceptions and

---

[14] John 4:34; 8:28-29; and others.

[15] John 21:15-17; *phileō* versus *agapaō.*

[16] Deut 30:19-20; Matt 22:36-37; 1 John 4:16.

teach us to care about others in addition to loving ourselves and our families.[17] This includes going well past the norm of our societies and even learning to care about our enemies (Matt 5:43-48).

It was not long after the start of the Creation that Satan called God a liar regarding death (separation from God) through disobedience and tempted Eve and Adam to sin against God resulting in their immediate separation from Him (spiritual death: Gen 3:1-6, 24). This was the start of our present fallen world.

Everyone starts with a corrupted nature due to Adam and Eve's initial sin and the additional sins committed over hundreds and hundreds of years by those who have gone before us. Then, we add the consequences of our personal sins to the mix. This corruption is shared by all on some level, and, therefore, sin affects all.

But, as we look at the world and our fallen nature and compare it to the purity of our loving Creator, some of us have come to a point in our lives that we want a change for the better. We want a pure godly life and, therefore, we have called out for a savior.

What complicates matters further is not only the fact that all are born into sin, but, in reality, we are all born into an ongoing war initiated by Satan against God.[18] God could have locked Satan up at any time even prior to or during the Creation, and eventually, He will do just that (Rev 20:10). But, it is clear from God's Word that God allows Satan to remain present to tempt us to rebel against Him in order to force us to think about our own fallen nature, His goodness, and the future sinless New Heaven and New Earth.

We should also keep in mind that God's Anointed Messiah, Jesus, did not come to bring peace to the whole world but instead to divide it between those who are willing to follow God and His

---

[17] Matt 22:39; 25:34-40; John 13:34.

[18] Matt 11:12; 1 Peter 5:8-11; Rev 12:7-11.

righteous ways and those who are not.[19] Although we do not presently have world peace, let's thank God that Jesus came to bring eternal peace to all who learn to listen to Them (Eph 2:14-16).

God has a continuous open door policy for all who voluntarily submit to His lordship forgiving and removing our sin and reconciling us into His eternal holy family through a second birth, a spiritual birth. So, as we continue to reflect on God and His goodness, we come to realize that He expects us to listen to Him because He is our creator and father, who loves us beyond our comprehension and constantly works on our behalf. Everything that He wants to teach us is for our personal and collective good. God teaches us that true joy and inner peace come from dying to our self-centered selfish aspirations and joining Him in serving one another.

Being part of God's eternal intimate loving righteous family brings about joy and inner peace that cannot be duplicated by any perversion of God's way of life. Jesus wants our joy to be full, which can only be accomplished by following Him. As we follow God's leadership and allow Him to transform us, the Holy Spirit helps us to become more and more like Jesus, which helps us grow in love, joy, peace, patience, kindness, goodness, faithfulness, gentleness, and self-control (Gal 5:22-23; cf. 1 Cor 13).

Born To Die Once & Then the Judgement

> **Just as it is determined (appointed) for men to die once, but after this judgment . . . .**
>
> **Hebrews 9:27**

All people live out the physical portion of their eternal life ***only one time***, and all of us will be judged for our actions during this time period of our life, if we don't start following Jesus. There is no reincarnation allowing us a second chance to accept God's love and righteousness. With our God-given abundant free will,

---

[19] Matt 10:34-39; Luke 12:49-53.

let's make good eternal choices and meet the needs of others as God leads.

From the moment that we are physically conceived, we have eternal existence. Then, God begins developing those of us who listen throughout this physical stage of our eternal life until He says that ***it is finished!*** Through Scriptures, we know that a time is coming when God will manifest to all Creation those individuals who have learned to truly love Him with His caring righteous ways.[20] In Scripture, God's revelation of those who learn to love Him is called by several names including His call, choice, and/or election.

If one never commits to follow Jesus, he cannot bring character witnesses before God for the Great White Throne Judgement.[21] God has perfect knowledge of everyone's inner motives and exposes the truth of each person's love and righteousness or lack of it to all Creation. God is solely responsible to expose the true character of all who do not receive Him into their lives.

May times, our selfish desires cause us to favor ourselves over others during our initial development. In addition, our self rationalization due to selfishness and its corresponding disobedience to God distorts reality. Our disobedience against God's will has even distorted our collective sense of right and wrong throughout the various levels of our twentieth-first century Western Civilization, and many have turned their back on God's social order and desire for our lives.

Collectively within our societies, many have come to an extreme position against God to include condoning the killing of our unborn children (abortion) and casting aside God's family values. In addition, many are ignoring or taking part in human trafficking, causing social division for political gain, and are looking the other way or encouraging other biological perversion to

---

[20] Rom 8:18-19, 28-30; 1 Cor 2:9; James 1:12; 2:5; 1 Peter 1:2-5.

[21] Rev 20:11-15; 21:7-8.

include sanctioning same-sex marriages, sex changes and other sexual perversion such as men playing in woman's sports.

Jesus makes us vividly aware that the ability to know good and to do good comes only from our Heavenly Father.[22] He is good and all good comes from Him. Therefore, we need the Creator to help us evaluate our motives for everything that we do. Anytime that we consciously or subconsciously place ourselves, our families, or other organizations above others, we no longer see the world as God intended. His actions and words tell us that He created all of us equal in being– not ability –and wants everyone to spend eternity with Him.

We should be mourning for those who are hurting just as an individual laments for a lost loved one.[23] This pain should compel us to act. We cannot be complete nor at peace without the help of Jesus Christ. We must learn to love God and others and turn to Him for proper development and guidance.[24]

Jesus was sent by the Father for one main purpose: to save us from ourselves and the Evil One.[25] God exposes our self-centeredness, selfishness, and corresponding disobedience so that we might know ourselves and turn to Him for proper development. If we will allow it, He will help us become whole so that we can live in peace with Him and each other. As we allow God to develop us, it becomes ***easier . . . and easier . . . and easier*** to ask Him for forgiveness of our wrongdoing. It becomes easier each time that we come to Him in our imperfection confessing our wrongdoing and seeking help to do better the next time.[26]

---

[22] Matt 19:17; Luke 18:19; John 20:17.

[23] Matt 5:4. God is longsuffering: Exod 34:6; Num 14:18; Rom 2:4; 1 Tim 1:16; 2 Peter 3:9, 15.

[24] Isaiah 29:13; Psalm 51.

[25] James 1:14-15; John 3:16-17, 10:10; Matt 1:21 (John 1:10-11); 18:11; Luke 9:56.

[26] 1 John 3:9 and others.

From the time that Adam and Eve initially disobeyed God, disobedience has separated all of us from a ***perfect-fellowship*** with God and each other.[27] When Adam and Eve disobeyed God and then hid from Him, God sent them from His presence. Their sin produced shame and fear causing both of them to hide themselves from Him. Disobedience to God had changed their ability to live in perfect unity with a loving righteous Father, and therefore, they died spiritually being separated from God's immediate presence.

Although this initial disobedience and loss of perfect fellowship causes all of us much pain, our Heavenly Father knew what He was doing from the very beginning before He initiated His perfect plan of Creation through its physical implementation. His willingness to pay the supreme cost of giving His creation an abundant free will demonstrates His desire to create an equalitarian righteous family full of love and grace. This fact should encourage all people to receive Him into their lives in order to live forever in peace and harmony within His holy family.

Through the Cross, Jesus ultimately brings all who listen into a perfected caring relationship with God.[28] If we are willing to learn to trust and obey God because of His great fairness and love, He promises to help us become mature and immediately starts to live in a closer interactive relationship with us.[29]

Once we commit to following Jesus, we become immediately reconciled to God, and He begins our moral transformation process promising us that there is coming a day when His perfected creation will be realized. When that happens, God's obedient children will be with Him and their moral character will be fully transformed to be like Jesus'.[30]

---

[27] Rom 3:23.

[28] God's Foreknowledge and Plan: Matt 25:34; Eph 1:4; Col 1:12-20; 2 Tim 1:9; 1 Peter 1:18-20; Rev 13:8. God's Salvation: John 3:16-17; Heb 2:9-17; 9:12-15; 2 Cor 5:17-21; Col 2:13-14.

[29] Eph 1:13-14; John 14; cf. John 5:24; Rom 8:1; 1 John 3:2.

[30] Phil 1:6; Rom 8:28-29; 1 John 3:1-3.

At that time, God's righteous children will no longer be ashamed nor afraid due to their past wrongdoings because Jesus' atoning work on a cross will have removed all of their bad actions (sins); Jesus made our sins His own on the Cross of Calvary.[31] Therefore, those of us who are following Jesus can approach His throne with great joy without worrying about past sin (Rom 5:1-5; Phil 1:20; 1 John 2:28).

At the moment that an individual truly decides to follow Jesus Christ from the heart,[32] they are born from above and fully reconciled into our Heavenly Father's family.[33] With immediate reconciliation comes ***less . . . and less . . . and less . . .*** disobedience over time. With our reconciliation, we start our individual accelerated process of maturing under Jesus' leadership. God increases our love for Him and all people, and our growing love for God and others calls us into ***action***.

Scripture tells us that those who accept God's love and righteousness do not sin continually.[34] The Greek language that our New Testament Scripture was written in is easier to understand regarding the continual action of sin. It conveys the thought that we are ***not*** to be ***continually . . . continually . . . continually*** sinning. Continual sinning makes us want to hide ourselves and our actions from our Heavenly Father and one another. How do we stop our continual sinning? We must truly learn to trust God and allow Him to teach us to love Him and one another as we continually read His Word and seek His help in responding properly to what we learn.

Through God's ongoing perfecting of our love, we will sin less and less over time. Remember, God created us for a mature, perfect interactive relationship with Him and one another. Jesus taught that all of the Law and the Prophets can be summed through

---

[31] Heb 1:2-3; Gal 3:13-14; Col 2:13-14: 2 Cor 5:21; 1 Peter 2:24.

[32] Rom 10:9-10.

[33] Born From Above: John 3:3-5; Eph 1:13-14; 1 Peter 1:22-23. Being God's Children: John 17:20-23; Eph 1:4-5, 13-14; Rom 8:14-17.

[34] 1 John 3:9.

two commandments: love God to the best of our ability, and love each other as He loves us.[35]

God tells us through His Word in many places including through the Law and the Prophets that His desire is fulfilled when we truly learn to care about each other. In addition, He tells us that if we do not love those around us, we do not really love Him.[36] Let us all strive to follow Jesus' one new commandment, which is to love one another as He loves us.[37] Thinking about the good that God has done for us should bring forth a desire in us to learn to return His love and learn to love one another as He loves us.

But beware, our development will not come easily. In addition to the existence of a righteous-loving Creator and a multitude of loving individuals, part of us wants things our way and is encouraged by Satan, who is in direct defiance of God and is literally at war with Him trying to take over His Kingdom.

Satan exalted himself above God and all others before the Creation and has been trying continually to take over God's position of authority ever since. He is self-centered and uses every kind of deception possible in his war against our Heavenly Father and us.[38] In his war to overpower God, this self-appointed dictator has been using deception and our own selfishness to tempt us to turn from our Heavenly Father and His good way of life.[39]

Satan uses our own selfishness and pride to deceive, distract, and disable us from doing the good work that our Father wants us to do. In addition, Satan uses our self-centeredness to divide us into the smallest possible groups. Keep in mind that Jesus warned us that a kingdom divided against itself will fall (Matt 12:25; Mark 3:24-25; Luke 11:17).

---

[35] Matt 22:37-40.

[36] 1 John 4:20; cf. Gal 5:13-14.

[37] John 13:34; 15:12-13.

[38] 1 John 3:8; Eph 6:10-12; Rev 12:7-17.

[39] John 8:44; 2 Cor 11:13-15; James 1:13-15.

If Satan could make us think that we are islands unto ourselves, he would do so. This is exactly opposite God's desire for us to learn to work together and love everyone equally. God's written Word reminds us that if we are followers of Jesus, we are united through Jesus and each of us make up part of the whole.[40]

Jesus has also warned us that Satan comes only to steal, kill, and destroy and lets us know that an abundant fulfilling life comes only from our Heavenly Father.[41] During this short portion of our eternal life, God does everything possible except taking away our free will to awaken us to His desired eternal life. As soon as we start listening to Him, He begins developing us into mature caring social beings. If we do not listen to our loving Heavenly Father, we face the painful consequences of a less fulfilling life now and in the future eternal judgment, separation from God, pain, and shame.[42]

The Ultimate Victory Is Obtained through Following Jesus

As we consider our individual eternal outcomes, let's keep in mind that God's finalized Creation has only two final outcomes and all people end up with one or the other: (1) living eternally sinless caring lives within the New Heaven and New Earth with God and other loving righteous beings; or (2) living with our bad actions (sin) eternally separated from God with eternal judgment and shame within a prison commonly called Hell or the Lake of Fire.[43] Knowing this should help us consider carefully what we really want now and for eternity.

At the beginning of the Creation, after Eve and Adam sinned against God partaking of the Tree of the Knowledge of

---

[40] Rom 12:5; 1 Cor 1:10-13; 12; Eph 4:4-7, 13-16.

[41] John 10:10; 1 Peter 5:6-9.

[42] Dan 12:2; Matt 25:41-46; Rev 20:11-15; 21:8.

[43] Rev 20:11-21:8.

Good and Evil, all people have been born within God's Creation with a marred personality that has some degree of self-centeredness, selfishness, and pride.[44] Adam and Eve had abundant free will and had to make important decisions (choices) throughout their physical lives, and so do we!

Within God's overall Creation, abundant free will is a critically important gift given to everyone because God wants a free interaction with everyone. ***He is not creating robots!*** Good choices produce good eternal outcomes; bad choices lead to pain and suffering. If God and His ways do not become acceptable sometime during our physical lives, one's bad choices lead to an eternal prison sentence within Hell.

If we keep in mind that God wants everyone to become a member of His voluntary eternal righteous family, that fact should help everyone consider more carefully God's fantastic invitation to be part of His eternal family. But, with our less than perfect personalities and Satan's ongoing encouragement and deception aimed at moving everyone away from God, we should all listen carefully when God presents us with times of spiritually awakening aimed at helping us know reality so that we will make good decisions (choices).

Most people are engaged in some form of busyness, therefore it is very important to listen when God provides special moments of enlightenment.[45] If one ignores God in order to live life the way that they want, they will be forfeiting the very best life now and for eternity.

So, what is the highest form of success that anyone can achieve during his or her physical life? The ultimate success or victory that anyone can achieve is accepting God's invitation to join His family and receiving Him as both lord and savior due to a growing love for Him and fellow man.[46]

---

[44] Gen 3; Rom 5:12-19; cf. Rom 3:21-24.

[45] Rom 1:16-2:16.

[46] Rev 3:18-21; 21:7; 22:1-5; cf. John 14:23-24.

Normally, many have an inner battle over whether or not they will give up personal lordship over God's leadership. Even when someone realizes that God is really good and only wants the best for everyone, it is still hard to let go of personal desires and embrace the world from God's perspective learning to care about everyone. When someone comes to that place and turns from their own ways to follow God and His way of life, spiritual birth into His family occurs and nothing can every remove them from His eternal family from that moment on.[47]

Most people know that God loves them beyond their comprehension but still struggle internally to allow Him to be lord over all aspects of their lives. Even knowing that God only wants the best for all people, it is still hard for most to allow Him to have the final say. So for many, they have to struggle with personal desires and weigh those desires against God's desire for their lives. If they weigh this carefully, some will figure out that God is worthy to follow and will then want God to help them develop properly. Once one starts following Jesus, they enter into a special ongoing process called "sanctification."[48] Over time, God trains His children in righteous living and leads them into their assigned good works.[49]

Making the Best Choice for Eternity

> **Enter through the narrow gate, because the gate is wide and the way that is leading into destruction is broad, and those who are leading themselves through it (the wide gate) are many– because the gate is narrow and the way that leads into the Life**

---

[47] John 3:3, 5, 14-17; Rom 8:28-39; 10:9; Eph 1:13-14; etc.

[48] Sanctification is an ongoing process whereby God develops His children day by day into a holier and holier life style; Rom 6:22; trust & obey=born again: John 3:3-5, 14-17; Rom 10:9.

[49] Eph 2:10; cf. Matt 25:34-40; 28:18-20.

> **has been made narrow (difficult); indeed those who are discovering it (the narrow gate) are few.**
> **Matt. 7:13-14**

Our Heavenly Father gives everyone abundant free will and asks everyone ***to seek*** Him for cleansing from the past and development for the future.[50] In demonstrating His incredible love for all through the planned death of His Son on a cross, He has given everyone proof of His sincere desire for full, sinless, mature fellowship with as many as will listen to Him.

Because of His righteous nature and great love for us, we should subordinate our will to His and allow Him to develop us.[51] He warns everyone that there are only two paths in reality. If we follow the broad path, which is the sum of all paths other than following Jesus, we will ultimately lose the eternal godly love, joy, and peace that God has in store for us. This path to destruction is wide and easy to follow especially if we have friends traveling it. Doing wrong with friends does not seem as bad to us as doing wrong alone. Therefore, be careful about whom you pick as friends and what you do with them.

This wide path leading to destruction is laden with self-centered, selfish, prideful individuals. Although the wide path leading to destruction may have its moments of pleasure, a person pays a terrible price if he or she stays on it by losing one's opportunities to join God in His good work and losing one's place in God's eternal holy family.

Jesus Christ teaches us that all goodness, which is derived from God's love, comes from God alone; God is the source of love and love's corresponding goodness for all including Jesus' goodness.[52] Those who truly seek God and His will for their lives

---

[50] Seek & Find: Matt 6:33; 7:7-8, 14; Luke 11:9-10.

[51] Some of God's prophets used the metaphorical imagery of the potter and clay to illuminate this idea (Isa 64:8; Jer 18:1-6).

[52] Luke 18:18-19; 1 John 4:8,10,16,19.

will find their individual narrow path to eternal life through Jesus.[53] Following Jesus is the path to eternal life with God; He is the ***only*** Way to the Father,[54] and all other so-called "paths to God" are part of the Broad Path/Road of Destruction that many follow.

We will never have inner peace if we blatantly violate the very reason that God created us, which was to have a pure-caring relationship with Him and one another. If we continue to ignore God's love and authority living mainly for ourselves, our own families, or any other group(s) other than the Family of God, our hearts will eventually become so hardened that we will never want to join God for eternity.

Because God desires us to want to be in His family (free will) and live with Him and one another in a caring righteous manner, He will not force any of us to do so. He desires a ***free-willed*** multi-personal relationship with everyone. God warns us that living in a self-centered, selfishness state of mind with its corresponding disobedience does not allow us to be developed properly and prohibits us from spending eternity with Him.[55] Therefore, we must learn to listen to God, or our separation will become so complete that we will feel an emptiness that is hard to comprehend. Scripture says that this emptiness and eventual extreme pain causes "wailing and gnashing of teeth."[56]

Although the Father suffered great agony over His Son's rejection and death, both knew that they were making ***the right way possible*** for us to be with them forever. We know that this is true through Nature and the confirming consistent work of the

---

[53] John 7:17; 8:31-36; live out the assigned good works (Eph 2:10).

[54] John 14:6; Acts 4:12; 1 Tim 2:3-5.

[55] The prodigal son needed something to happen in his life to show him the difference between godly love and selfishness (Luke 15).

[56] Matt 13:41-50; 25:41-46, Rev 19:20; 20:11-15. Observe that in Matt 8:12, God's disobedient children will be cast into darkness vs. fire with light. Through metaphorical imagery, God gives everyone a glimpse of the pain that eternal separation from Him and judgment for bad actions brings.

Holy Spirit in everyone's lives.[57] Their combined demonstration of genuine love and persistent encouragement should draw us to them. As we learn to listen to God, He cleanses us from our sins and draws us into His good works.

As we learn to obey Jesus, we begin to stand upon our Father's promises. As we start walking with God, we start to develop a trust for His perfect plan of godly love and corresponding unity, and we join Him in His Great Work of Love, the Creation. We take great comfort in knowing that we will truly experience the best life now and obtain perfection after death,[58] living in a sinless world where there will no longer be pain and sorrow.[59]

---

[57] Rom 1:20-22; John 16:7-11.

[58] Phil 1:6; Rom 8:29; 1 John 3:1-3.

[59] Rev 21:1-7.

Chapter 2
Jesus Is Lord!

Jesus, "You (my disciples) are proclaiming me, The Teacher and The Lord, and you are speaking correctly, for I am." John 13:13

Now, let the Holy Spirit, the Spirit of Truth, help us realize more fully who is encouraging, instructing, and leading those who listen.[60] This great teacher and leader is the Son of the living God.[61] He is working in perfect godly unity with the Father and Holy Spirit. Jesus teaches us reality so that we may mature and become free from bondage caused by our own selfishness. Jesus Christ is ***not*** just another good man; Jesus is ***not*** just another great prophet; Jesus Christ ***is*** the son of the Living God who worked in close unity with His father putting together the total Creation including the heavens, Earth, and humanity.[62] Jesus is the power who is literally holding the Creation together.[63] The Father has appointed Jesus, our Eldest Brother, to lead us for eternity.[64]

---

[60] John 14:23, "...We will come...," 26; 16:7-14.

[61] Matt 16:16. According to Jesus, no one is to be proclaimed "leader" except Him (Matt 23:10).

[62] Matt 16:13-17; John 1:3,10; Eph 2:10; Col 1:12-22; Heb 1:2.

[63] Col 1:17.

[64] Eph 1:19-21.

Jesus' Farewell Discourse and Prayer

Jesus' farewell discourse and prayer is different in one very important aspect from all other leadership farewells recorded in God's Word. In His farewell discourse, Jesus never relinquishes His authority to a successor. After completing His last supper with them, Jesus speaks to His disciples before going to the Cross. He knows that He is responsible to continue teaching and leading all who are willing to trust and obey Him. John gives us this account of Jesus' commandments and exhortations to His disciples and His requests to the Father for His disciples of all ages in John 13-17. Let us begin looking at Jesus' ***continued*** lordship by examining His farewell discourse and prayer comparing it to other biblical farewell discourses.

The practice of commandment, exhortation, and prayer for one's loved ones at the point of death is a well-attested practice. Being responsible for the lives of their loved ones, the authority figure passes on his most valuable thoughts and concerns for those who will follow him. Before a final prayer or blessing, the last set of instructions and exhortations normally includes confirmation of the next authority figure, the one who is going to assume responsibility for the guidance and care of the family or nation. Three examples from the Bible are: (1) Isaac's blessing of Jacob;[65] (2) Israel's (Jacob's) commandments and blessings to his sons and their families who made up the original families known as the nation of Israel;[66] and (3) Moses' exhortations, commandments, and prayer for the blessing of each tribe of Israel.[67] In the Gospel of John, we see Jesus engaging in the same action. In His farewell discourse, Jesus gives His disciples one new commandment, "Love

---

[65] Gen 27:2, 27-30.

[66] Gen 48-49.

[67] Deut 1-4, 32; 5-31; and Deut 33 respectively.

one another just as I have loved you."[68] He also exhorts and encourages, "Let not your heart be troubled,[69] for we (Jesus and the Father) will come to you through another Comforter, the Spirit of Truth."[70]

The one ***major*** difference between Jesus' farewell discourse and prayer and all of the other biblical farewells is that Jesus never relinquished His authority as the highest leader of the Church to another individual. Although dying leaders normally appointed new leaders to take their place, Jesus deliberately did not appoint a new leader, because He expected to become the ***risen*** Lord in just three days. And He knew that after His ascension, He would continue to teach and lead His people through the Spirit of Truth. Jesus said,

> **I shall not leave you orphans; I am coming to you. Yet a little while, and the world will no longer observe me, but you (pl) will observe me; because I am alive, indeed you shall live also. In that day you will know that I am in my Father, and you in me, and I in you . . . 26 But the Comforter, the Holy Spirit, whom the Father shall send in my name, He will teach you all things, and He shall remind you of all that I spoke to you. I am leaving peace for you; I am giving you my peace; not as the world gives do I give to you. Let not your heart be troubled nor afraid. John 14:18-27**

---

[68] John 13:34; 15:12, 17.

[69] John 14:1.

[70] John 14:16-17; in addition, see John 14:6, 18, 20, 26-27.

Jesus Christ Is the Son of the Living God

Our eldest brother **is** the first son of the living God.[71] He is working in perfect unity with the Father. Yes, Jesus Christ is **not** just another good man nor is He just another great prophet; Jesus Christ **is** the son of the Living God who helped His father with our creation.[72] We can learn a lot about our savior and His great qualifications to lead us through Paul's letter to the Colossians.

Jesus Christ is the ***Beloved Son*** of the Father who has redeemed us from our sins (Col 1:13-14); Jesus is loved tremendously by the Father. Jesus is the ***Image of God***, and God cannot be seen with human eyes,[73] yet we can see the Father's nature by observing Jesus.[74] He is the ***Firstborn*** having the rights of the firstborn over every creature (Col 1:15), yet He shares His rights with every Believer.[75]

Jesus is the ***Master Craftsman***,[76] creating all things seen and unseen in Heaven and on Earth. We were created through Jesus for fellowship with Jesus (Col 1:16).[77] Jesus is the Word,[78] the

---

[71] Matt 16:16.

[72] Matt 16:13-17; John 1:3,10; Eph 2:10; Heb 1:2.

[73] John 14:7 (We can see the Father through Jesus Christ); 1 John 4:12, 20: No one on Earth has seen the Father except Christ.

[74] John 12:45; 14:9.

[75] John 1:14 . . . 17:5 . . . 17:22.

[76] John 1:10; Eph 2:10, "For we are His (God's) workmanship, having been created in/through Christ Jesus for good works. . .; Heb 1:2.

[77] 1 John 1:3.

[78] John 1:3, 10.

Origin, the Source, from which the Creation came.[79] Jesus was before all,[80] ***the Eldest***, and it is ***through Him*** that all things continue. Literally, Jesus has set the Creation in motion and is continuing to hold it together (Col 1:17).

Jesus is the ***Head*** of the Body, the Church,[81] and sits at the right hand of the Father in power forever.[82] Jesus is the beginning of resurrected life, the ***Firstborn from the Dead***. Because Jesus is the oldest son, the first, and continues to obey our Father faithfully, He has the greatest eternal responsibility and corresponding authority over all things (Col 1:18).[83]

Jesus is the ***Sinless Reconciler***, reconciling us and *those in Heaven* to the Father through the Cross (Col 1:19-20).[84] Prior to the Creation, our Heavenly Father and Jesus agreed together to make an atonement for our disobedience.[85]

The Father sent Jesus, the prophesied Messiah (Christ), to die on the Cross for all people, and then He raised Jesus from the dead and set Him over all powers and authorities in Heaven and on Earth forever. Today, this same Jesus delivers all who will come to trust and obey Him from the power of the Evil One.[86]

---

[79] Rev 3:14.

[80] John 1:1.

[81] Eph 1:22-23; 4:15; 5:23; Rom 12 and 1 Cor 12 discuss the Body.

[82] Eph 1:20-21.

[83] 1 Peter 3:22.

[84] Eph 1:7-10; Corinthians 5:17-21; Heb 9:22.

[85] Matt 25:34; Eph 1:4; 2 Tim 1:9; 1 Peter 1:19-20; Rev 13:8.

[86] John 10:10.

Jesus ***is*** the Son of the one true living God.[87] During Jesus' earthly ministry, many Jewish leaders ***ignored*** His identity and ***rejected*** His authority ***because of their hardened hearts toward God.***[88] Their hearts had become hardened as they took matters into their own hands and stopped listening to God. They would not give up control over their fellow man, which they had wrongfully taken from God.[89] Therefore, Jesus removed all of their responsibility and corresponding authority including what He had originally given them.[90] Their Temple was destroyed and they were driven out of Jerusalem approximately thirty five to forty years after Jesus' death and resurrection. Throughout time since Jesus' earthly ministry, many have continued to ***ignore*** His identity and ***reject*** His authority because of hardened hearts wanting things their own way.

Those who hear and receive Jesus Christ hear and receive the Father; those who hear and receive Jesus' disciples hear and receive Jesus.[91] The Father clearly spoke through Jesus during His earthly ministry, and presently Jesus is speaking to all who listen through the Holy Spirit, Scripture, and His Body, the Church.[92]

---

[87] Matt 16:16 (the Christ, the Son of the Living God); Mark 8:29 (the Christ); John 6:69 (the Holy One of God).

[88] Jesus proclaims His identity through His words and actions: John 5:17, 19; 17:1. His Rejection: Matt 26:63; Mark 14:61; Luke 22:70; John 5:18; 19:7. Hardened Hearts: Matt 13:13-15.

[89] Matt 21:33-39.

[90] John 8:31-47; Matt 21:43 (Kingdom taken from religious authorities); John 3:35; 5:22-23 (honor the Son), 30 (Jesus' seeks the Father's will); 17:2; Eph 1:21.

[91] Matt 10:40; Mark 9:37b; Luke 9:48b; John 12:44; Gal 4:14.

[92] Jesus teaches us the Father's will (Heb 1:2; John 8:28, 47; 17:8). During this age, the Church is the Light to the World: Eph 3:10. In addition to the Father & Son being with us now through the Holy Spirit, we have God's written Word and the same Holy Spirit who originally helped the original writers write it helping us to understand it. We are to

God's Word Guarantees Inner Peace and Joy

> **Come to me all who are laboring and are burdened, and I will give you relief. Take up my yoke upon yourselves and learn from me, because I am gentle and humble in heart, and you will find relief for your souls. For my yoke is merciful and my burden is light (easy to bear).**[93]
>
> **Matthew 11:28-30**

Because God truly cares for us, He asks us to give Him our anxieties, trading our heavy burdens for lighter loads. There is inner peace and joy for every individual who allows the Creator to guide his or her life.[94] God teaches all who learn to love Him that there is something much greater than self, a pure non-selfish interrelationship with God ***and*** other obedient members of His family. Jesus leads us through a learning experience that transforms our lives forever. He teaches us to love all people, and we learn to live as family members of God ministering to all.

Families are social units that should provide proper development and support. The family's primary role is to provide each new member of society, the child, with its core training in social skills and moral behavior. This training becomes part of that member's very being, their "inner self." The family continues to provide support for its members throughout all phases of life.

A biblical family structure on Earth is similar to God's eternal family structure. A husband is to love his wife as Jesus loves the Church. Therefore, a husband should learn to love his wife to the point of being willing to lay down his life to save her.

---

allow God to speak through us to the World– Evangelism: Matt 10:20 & Mark 13:11; Christian Defense: Matt 10:20 & Mark 13:11.

[93] Luke 4:18-21; Isaiah 61:1-2.

[94] John 17:13, 23; Rom 5:1-5.

Jesus put his love for us into action; He died for us and continues to lead us!

A husband must learn to consider his wife's welfare as important or more than his own. A husband is never a dictator just as Jesus is not a dictator. Men must allow ***free will*** to work within their families just as God allows ***abundant free will*** to influence all humanity. In response to her husband's love, a wife is to submit to the authority of her husband and help him in every way possible. Although women are to submit to the authority of their husbands, they are not inferior to men in any way. God tells us clearly that all men and women of all nationalities and walks of life are equal to each other through Jesus Christ.[95] Jesus has made us ***free*** and ***equal family members*** through His death on a cross.

The family of God is continually developed and directed through Jesus by our Heavenly Father. There cannot be peace in any organization without some form of order including levels of authority. We cannot be complete individually or corporately with its accompanying joy without allowing God to prepare us for our proper places in His family. If we listen to God, He will prepare us for our individual positions within His family. As we become people of grace and righteousness, God gives us more and more responsibility to help in His ministry to all. When we learn to listen to God, we begin a relationship with Him and others that provides both internal and eternal peace.[96]

We ***are*** children of God and have been called into a fantastic relationship that makes us equal family members with Jesus. We ***are*** loved by the Father as Jesus is loved, and we are coheirs with Him in everything.[97] Yet, we are clearly not equal with Jesus in responsibilities or authority: Jesus ***is*** our lord forever.

As we learn to trust and obey God, Jesus shares some of His responsibility and authority with us.[98] We learn to work with

---

[95] Matt 22:28-30; Gal 3:26-29; 1 Peter 3:7.

[96] Love: John 3:16-17; 1 John 4:20; Peace: Rom 5:1-5; Phil 4:4-7.

[97] Rom 8:14-17; 1 Peter 3:7; Rev 21:7.

[98] 1 Peter 2:9; Acts 1:8; Rev 3:21.

Him in many ways ministering to people in our communities and all over the world.

God does not call all people into full-time ministry, but He does ask all people to join Him in a full-time relationship. He gives us the resources, talent, and frame of mind to carry out the good works that He established from the beginning of the Creation for us.[99] Whatever good work God has established for you, feel assured that He has also provided abundantly the empowerment, resources, talent, and frame of mind needed for you to complete the work.[100]

Repentance: Turning from Self to God

Being a child of God starts with a spiritual awakening that leads to repentance and corresponding commitment. Satan does his best to keep all people busy, confused, and focused on themselves. God continually works in peoples' minds and hearts to bring them to a place where they recognize the reality of His love and the destructive nature of self-centeredness and selfishness (spiritual awakening).[101] For some, God is able to reach them during some of their quieter moments; for others God has to set up or allow trials in order to produce spiritual awakenings through a crises.[102] In all cases, God does not want anyone to be eternally separated from Him; He patiently works with everyone wanting all to come to the point of repentance (turning from self to Him) so that they will turn to Him for salvation and an eternal place in His family (2 Peter 3:9).

---

[99] Eph 2:10; Titus 2:14. Our good works include exposing and correcting wrongdoing (1 Cor 6:1-5).

[100] Acts 1:8; Eph 1:19; 3:14-20; Phil 4:13.

[101] Rom 1:18–2:16.

[102] One example is the account of the self-centered son (Prodigal Son: Luke 15:11–32) who through a major crisis finally came to understand reality; he came to himself, his senses (Luke 15:17).

But beware! Jesus was clear, many stay on the wide road of self-centeredness and selfishness that leads to eternal shame and suffering and only a few turn off onto the narrow way of life that leads to repentance and corresponding commitment, which results in spiritual birth into God's eternal close-knit holy family.[103] Not only does Jesus stand at the door of everyone's life asking to be part of it, He asks us to seek and follow Him.[104]

If we would be honest with one another, most of us would admit that we want things our own way and want everything to be as easy as possible. Scripture is clear that God is longsuffering and has been working hard on humanity's behalf from the very beginning. The Son of God, Jesus Christ, working with His Father died both physically and spiritually in order to provide a way for good to triumph over evil for all eternally. ***Through Jesus' spiritual death, He experienced separation from the Father for the first time in eternity due to our sin (bad actions) being made part of His life,*** so that those who were trusting God would never experience spiritual death even for one second.[105] Jesus provided a way to personally take on our bad actions, which gives those who submit to God a sinless past when entering into God's presence.[106]

John the Baptist started his ministry declaring that everyone needed to "repent." Jesus started His earthly ministry telling all to "repent." The Early Church proclaimed the need to "repent."[107] Without repentance, which is turning from self to God, one remains in a fallen self-centered selfish state of existence.

"Repentance" indicates a change of heart, which results in a change of one's life and life style, a turning from self and sin to

---

[103] Matt 7:13–14.

[104] Jesus: Rev 3:20; Us: Matt 7:7–8.

[105] John 11:25–26; Heb 2:9.

[106] Heb 1:2-3; Gal 3:13–14; 2 Cor 5:21; cf. Acts 2:27, 31; Col 2:13–14; 1 Peter 2:24.

[107] John: Matt 3:2; Jesus: Matt 4:17; the Early Church: Acts 2:38.

God and His righteous way of life.[108] ***Repentance triggers action.*** Repentance brings about a true commitment to stop living for self and start living for God and others. In reality, God knows everyone's heart and true repentance brings about conversion, which is when one is spiritually born into God's holy family, which is a work of God after genuine repentance.[109] ***Repentance with its corresponding commitment to submit to God's lordship and follow Jesus is the key to being born into God's eternal holy family!***

In Acts 26:19–20, Luke speaks of repentance being part of the process of "turning to" God. He recalled Paul telling King Agrippa that he, Paul, had been obedient to God's revelation to him, and therefore, he was proclaiming the Good News to many including the Gentiles telling them "to repent and turn to the (one true) God" ***doing works*** worthy of repentance.

Commitment & Discipleship

All who listen to God are commissioned by Him to represent Him as they become intentionally engaged in the spiritual battles going on all over the world for the eternal placement of each person.[110] God's children are not to sit on the sidelines. In fact, ***Jesus said that nobody is able to be one of His followers unless he or she is willing to deny self, pick up his or her cross daily, and follow Him*** into whatever battles He leads.[111] ***Nowhere in Scripture does God teach that someone can come to Him, pick up a pass to Heaven, ignore the battles going on around them, die physically, and have Jesus escort his or her spirit into Heaven.***

---

[108] See Joseph, *Experiencing Jesus' Joy*, 130-33, for more detail.

[109] John 1:12–13.

[110] Matt 5:13–10; 1 Peter 5:6–10; cf. John 15:1–2; 2 Cor 5:17–19; Eph 6:10–18.

[111] Luke 9:23; 14:26–27.

So ***why*** do so many people today make some sort of profession of faith and never experience the new creation "in Christ"?[112] In reality, ***without a genuine commitment to follow Jesus, there will be no spiritual birth into God's family and a realization of being a new creation.***

Satan has sold the world one of His biggest lies since the beginning of the Creation. ***Many believe that salvation is nothing more than obtaining a pass into heaven to be used when one dies.*** This lie causes people to think that they have to wait until they get to Heaven for anything to be better. ***What a lie!*** Sanctification, being molded and shaped by God, and good works starts immediately *for **all** who truly start following Jesus*.[113]

This new lie, which is being propagated by many proclaiming that everyone can pick up a pass leading into heaven by confessing their sins and claiming Jesus as their savior ***without following Him as lord***, is hindering many from considering a genuine commitment to follow Jesus. It is only through a turning from self and following Jesus (repentance with corresponding commitment) that one is saved from judgment as a sinner and spiritually born into God's family.

Spiritual renewal comes only from God according to His will and His rules.[114] Through spiritual birth into God's family comes the removal of sin and growth in God's righteousness. God's Word is clear, ***if individuals do not make true commitments to follow Jesus, they cannot be His disciples.***[115] Without making a true commitment to follow Jesus, there is no spiritual birth into God's eternal holy family. Heaven is only open to God's children and faithful heavenly beings.[116]

---

[112] 2 Cor 5:17.

[113] Rom 6:22; cf. Eph 2:10; Phil 2:13.

[114] John 1:13; 2 Peter 3:9.

[115] Luke 14:26–27.

[116] Rev 21:7–8, 27.

In addition to loss of eternal life, Satan's deceptions are causing many to live out unfulfilled lives instead of living fulfilled lives within God's family. Without spiritual rebirth, one lives without a personal relationship with God and misses out on a life filled with godly love, joy, and inner peace. It is only through repentance and corresponding commitment that one starts to experience the great joy of being part of God's family and working together with God and His family, the Church, to bring others into His eternal holy family for the best life now and forever.

Jesus' followers are being transformed,[117] and they are learning to love others as God loves all.[118] ***When they die physically, they do not need a pass into Heaven from anyone including church leaders because they are God's children.*** Heaven belongs to God ***and*** all of His children.[119] Jesus will meet them as they leave their physical bodies and escort them into the presence of their eternal Father (John 14:3; 1 John 3:1–2; Rev 21:3).

Beware, God will not be mocked![120] Each one of us will end up being judged according to our decisions and actions during this short physical portion of our eternal lives.[121] If you have never truly repented and made a corresponding commitment to follow Jesus' leading, now is a great time to do so. Make that commitment now. Tell God that you want to faithfully follow Jesus. He knows you and is waiting to receive you into His eternal loving righteous family.

---

[117] 2 Cor 5:17; Gal 5:22–23.

[118] 1 John 3:14; 4:16–19.

[119] John 14:1–3; 17:24; 20:17; Rom 8:17.

[120] Gal 6:7; cf. Luke 8:17; 16:15.

[121] Rom 2:11–16; 1 Peter 1:17. Compare the idea of life versus death as taught by God through Moses in Deut 28:12, 9, 15, and Moses' plea for Israel to "choose life" as shown in Deut 30:15–20.

Chapter 3
Experiencing Good & Evil Demands a Decision

Even if you have not yet come to a place of trusting God, it is highly probable that you have sensed an ongoing battle of evil trying to prevail over good. Most of us have come to realize that there is a way of life that is beneficial and many ways of life that ultimately bring harm to ourselves and others. The way that we live with others makes a real difference in the here-and-now and in the future. In reality, God has created the universe with real absolute standards for all life. When we follow His rules, we do good for ourselves and others, when we do not and go against God and His way of life, we harm ourselves and others. Because God is communicating to all, on some level, subconsciously or consciously, everyone is aware of God and His standards.[122]

Not only are most aware of the difference between good and evil, all participate in doing both. There is plenty of wrongdoing by all. No one is completely innocent. Everyone has fallen short of living out a perfectly righteous life according to God's standards *except Jesus Christ.*[123]

Evil is recognized by most societies around the world, and due to the harm done through evil actions, more time is spent keeping current on the latest evil than on good. Whether ignoring someone, speaking an unkind word, not helping someone whom God puts in our path, directly disobeying God's instructions for our lives, lying, cheating, stealing, killing, enslaving, sexually abusing, or doing some other form of evil, we all see and do some evil.

---

[122] Rom 1:18-32; 2:11-16.

[123] Heb 1:2-3; Rom 3:23; Isa 53:4-9; 2 Cor 5:21; 1 Peter 2:21-24.

Evil versus Good

Personally, we have all experienced times in our lives in which we have done something that has hurt someone else and have either felt immediate or eventual remorse. Even if someone has not been walking in spiritual awareness of God's presence and continual teaching, most recognize the fact that we all struggle with self-centered desires. Whether we listen to His leading or not, God talks to all and moves as many as listen into a place of awareness that helps make good choices easier.[124]

If we listen to God, He will help us look past our self-centered desires and block Satan's deceptions and noise. Satan's deceptions and noise are generated by many sources to include entertainment, technological gadgets, and even so-called friends at times. If we do not listen to God, we are controlled in some way by Satan, the Evil One. God desires to develop our individual consciences and teach each of us our assigned good works.[125] If we ignore or do not hear God's voice, it is easy to miss out on what is really going on including the blessings that come from living out our lives within God's will.

Even with those who are hostile toward God and His followers, God stays at work in everyone's life bringing as many as possible to a place of turning from self-centered lifestyles to Him and His righteous way of life for all. This turning is biblically called ***repentance***. God wants everyone to come to a place in his or her life that allows Him to teach them about His genuine concern and love for all, which in turn encourages many to come to Him for everyday help and eternal salvation.

Although many listen to God enough to know the difference between good and evil, there are many who have not listened well enough to know that ***our world is caught up in the middle of two powerful kingdoms at war:*** the Kingdom of God

---

[124] John 8:31b-32; 16:8-11.

[125] Phil 2:13; Eph 2:10; 1 Cor 12:18.

and the Kingdom of Hell presently ruled by Satan. God and His kingdom are more powerful and at the appropriate time will put Satan and his followers in an isolated place forever called Hell, the Lake of Fire, or Gehenna.

But, until that happens, God has been using Satan to force everyone to evaluate the good and evil around them and decide on which lifestyle they desire for eternity. Because all of us live out our lives doing and experiencing both good and evil, ***each has to decide*** if they want a close relationship with God and those who are listening to Him, or do they prefer to reject God's leadership and way of life not knowing that this alternative appears to give more freedom but in reality leads to a downward spiral toward eventual eternal shame, unrest, and suffering.

Satan is out to deceive as many as possible trying to keep them from listening to God so that they will never really get to know Him or His Word. God on the other hand, wants everyone to understand reality and consider carefully their future. When individuals start listening to God because of His great love and concern for all, He starts to mold and shape them into His own nature (likeness). On the other hand, for those who do not listen, God allows Satan to continue to deceive them into thinking that they are going to have an abundant joyful life *on their own terms*.

Whatever one ultimately decides determines one's ***eternal destiny***. No matter where you stand, you should stay alert knowing that our world is actually in the middle of a major spiritual war with eternal consequences and that God will eventually separate those who want to be with Him and His way of life from those who do not. God will rescue those who listen to Him from the long-term consequences of bad actions (sin).[126]

If you could look ahead in time and get a glimpse of both future kingdoms in their final states and see God and His perfected eternal sinless family living in love, peace, and joy, and Satan and those who follow in his footsteps continually hurting one another, what would you be willing to do for yourself and others in order to live with God and His family forever?

---

[126] Dan 12:2; cf. Matt 25:45-46; Rom 2:11-13; Gal 6:7; Rev 20:12.

In reality, God has already made a way for you to do this through Jesus Christ (John 14:6; Rom 1:16-17). If you really would like to know God better in order to follow Him, God will help you live out a more fulfilling life in the here-and-now experiencing His love, joy, and inner peace as part of your growing relationship with Him and other members of the Church.

Spiritual Warfare in General

> **From the days of John the Baptist until now, the Kingdom of the Heavens is suffering "violence," and "violent ones" are taking it by force.**[127]
> **Matt 11:12**

> **The Law and the prophets stood until John; from then the *Good News* of the Kingdom of God *is being proclaimed* and *everyone is "forcing himself through violence"* into *it.*[128] But, it is easier for the Heaven and Earth to pass away than for one stroke of a letter of the Law to fail.**
> **Luke 16:16-17**

Jesus said that He did not come into our world to produce world peace but instead division between those who would learn to follow Him and those who would not (Luke 12:49-51). And as noted directly above, Jesus also said that although many were trying to force their way into the Kingdom of Heaven, it would not happen. ***God has the final say and His conditions–given through the Law (God's instructions &commands) and prophets–will stand.*** It is easier for the heavens and the earth to be totally destroyed than for

---

[127] Greek *biazetai* representing "violence."

[128] Ditto: Greek *biazetai* representing "violence."

God's Word to fail.[129] It is clear through His Word, the Bible, that God's plans shall be accomplished without fail!

Everyone is trying to force their way into Heaven! Today, Satan is still at war with all of God's children blinding and deceiving as many as possible. As we keep in mind that all humanity is caught up in war between two kingdoms, God's and the rebels', keep in mind that Satan is a self-proclaimed dictator, who decided before the Creation to overthrow God, steal what He owns, and rule everything.[130] After Jesus' thousand-year reign toward the end of the Creation just for a brief moment, Satan will be allowed to lead once again those who are not listening to God. After this final rebellion, Satan will be permanently isolated from God and all righteous ones. He will be placed with other rebellious souls in the eternal Lake of Fire, which is commonly called Hell.[131]

It is clear from Scripture that God's Creation is full of bloody battles with Evil trying to overcome Good. John the Baptist died proclaiming that the Messiah and His Kingdom had come. Jesus died representing God as He demonstrated the love of God through His actions and words. Most of Jesus' main disciples died proclaiming the truth about God's plan of salvation for those who would follow Jesus. Over the centuries, thousands upon thousands have died as they followed Jesus through the guidance of the Holy Spirit.

As you study Scripture, you come to realize that our Heavenly Father has had everything under control from the very beginning. He sent Jesus into our world to teach us further revelation and then at just the right time, Jesus died for all. God teaches us that this battle between His Kingdom and the Kingdom of Hell will come to an end in God's perfect time when the Kingdom of Heaven is filled with God's new children. God's Kingdom is commonly called the Kingdom of Heaven, and

---

[129] Luke 16:16-17; cf. Isa 40:8; Matt 5:17-20.

[130] Matt 4:8-10; Eph 6:12.

[131] Rev. 20:7-10; cf. Rev 12:12; John 12:31; 16:11.

because of Jesus' redemptive work, it is also called the Kingdom of His Beloved Son, the Kingdom of Christ (Col 1:13; Eph 5:5).

As we consider our participation in the ongoing battle around us, we all must eventually ***make a decision*** regarding our ***eternal allegiance***. On this large battlefield called earth, there has been and continues to be many deceivers teaching many false concepts about the one true God, whose name is Yahweh, and His holy nature.

Keep in mind that there are many non-existent fabricated gods who stand in for Satan. They are presented to humanity as substitutes to replace Yahweh. *Satan uses these shadows of himself* to distort reality and keep people from knowing their loving Creator and His desire for an eternal mature close loving-kind (holy) family. Additional information on Satan's created gods and religious institutions can be studied through books such as Josh McDowell's *A Ready Defense.*[132]

God's Anointed One, Jesus, the true prophesied Messiah, came to lead people into God's light teaching reality and saving them from eternal separation from Their Creator. Jesus came bringing abundant life to all who listen here-and-now and for eternity (John 10:10). Jesus is the only access to our Heavenly Father (John 10:9; 14:6, Eph 2:18). If Jesus' followers stay focused on Him and follow Him, they will not be deceived so easily by Satan and will lead others into God's presence. But, as the battle for the souls of humanity continues on through the Creation process, we understand from God that there are many who will stay in the dark (keep things hidden) in order to do things for themselves at the expense of others, and we know that God will not force them to change. They must change on their own (abundant free will).[133]

---

[132] Josh McDowell, *A Ready Defense* (San Bernardino: Here's Life, 1990, reprint 1991).

[133] Matt 7:13; John 1:9-13; 3:19-20; 2 Thess 2:10-12.

Those who listen to God and start following Jesus are encouraged to put on the armor of God and resist evil:

> **From now on, *be continually strengthened in the Lord in the strength of His might.* Put on all of the armor of God in order to enable yourselves to stand before the scheming of the Devil, *because our battle is not against blood and flesh*, but instead against the leaders, the authorities, the cosmic powers of this darkness, the spirits of evil in the heavenly places. Eph 6:10-12**

Let's keep on reminding ourselves that we are part of God's creative work! As God enlarges His intimate close-knit holy family, Satan continually keeps fighting hard against Him and His growing family. In this ongoing fight, there was a strategic time when Satan encouraged Israel's religious leaders to crucify Jesus in order to silence Him, but to his surprise ***instead of getting rid of the Father's only Son, he unknowingly lost the battle to separate all of God's children from their Creator for eternity.*** Jesus' death on a cross made it possible for many sons and daughters to become part of God's eternal holy sinless family.

From the time of Jesus' death on the Cross and Satan's realization that he had lost the battle for the souls of all humanity, he has been doing his best to minimize God's victory. Satan has been distracting, placating, intimidating, and misleading as many people as possible so that they will not take the time to figure out what eternity will be like without God's presence (Rev 12:9, 12).

Over the centuries, God has been building His eternal family and filling His eternal Kingdom with loving righteous individuals. Over the same stretch of time, Satan has come to realize that his time is becoming shorter and shorter. Because of this, Satan has been working hard at escalating his attacks on humanity through deception and intimidation.

This Is Personal

If you are a committed follower of Jesus, have you ever wondered why some of the good things that you wish to do seem so difficult to start and accomplish although part of you knows that it should be easier? Does it seem that during the times when you want to do some good knowing that God has put something special in your heart, you seem to be swimming in molasses instead of water? If this is the case, you have experienced spiritual warfare firsthand. You may have come to realize that many of your own doubts and hesitations coupled with circumstances around you were ***not*** just part of the natural order of everyday life. In many cases, they were caused by acts of spiritual warfare against you and the godly actions that you were contemplating.

Satan and his followers are constantly trying to influence Jesus' followers looking for ways to hinder or stop completely what God has laid on their hearts. As God's children pray and seek His will for their individual and collective lives, they need to be aware–as Daniel was–that this ongoing battle is ultimately God's, as we do our individual parts. Keep in mind that God directly interacts in these ongoing battle and incorporates His angels to help Jesus' followers on an ongoing basis. And keep in mind that it is Jesus' followers joy, honor, and privilege to work under God's leadership as His ambassadors and priests (2 Cor 5:17-20; 1 Peter 2:9) awakening and rescuing those who will listen right up to the end of this Messianic Age.

This Is Ongoing

During the reigns of Darius, King of Chaldea, and Cyrus, King of Persia, God gave Daniel visions showing him future events (Dan 9-10). We see from Daniel's vision during the third year of Cyrus, that there was ongoing spiritual warfare just as today. One of Satan's angels, who was in a leadership position over Persia, had slowed one of God's angels down for 21 days until God's lead angel, Michael, came to his aid. Michael's intervention allowed God's assigned angel to go to Daniel and give him insight regarding His plans in all that was transpiring (Dan 10:12-14). This messenger from God stated that as soon as he had given Daniel God's vision, he was going right back to continue his fight against the same demonic leader in Persia as well as engage in a battle against one of Satan's angels who was heading up warfare in Greece (Dan 10:20). Even today, Satan consistently wages war with those who faithfully follow God.

Approximately five hundred years later, we learn that the same type of ongoing spiritual warfare was continuing. Paul stated that Satan had slowed him down when wanting to visit and encourage the Thessalonians whom he had led to the true Messiah (1 Thess 2:18). Satan is consistently waging war against God's obedient children causing as much stumbling, suffering, and damage as possible;[134] but if we listen to God, He will use our trials and tribulations to help others and build our individual character.

Daniel's account and Paul's warning about the bad angels who are helping Satan should be a warning for all of us. This ongoing war between good and evil has eternal consequences for all. Jesus did not ask our Heavenly Father to remove any of His followers from the evil of this world, but He did ask our Heavenly Father to protect His followers from the Evil One through His name (John 17:11b). Jesus' followers are part of His family and will be protected by God as part of His holy family. Whenever Jesus' followers fall short in any given battle or circumstance, God helps them do their part whether they physically live or die. The ultimate goal for Jesus' followers is to help as many as possible get to know God well enough to trust Him with their eternal lives out of a growing love for Him.

---

[134] e.g. 1 Thess 2:14-16; 3:4; 2 Thess 1:4-5; cf. Luke 16:13.

Spiritual Warfare & Satan's Deceptions

> **Do not be amazed, for *Satan transforms (disguises) himself as an angel of light.* Therefore, it is not a great thing if indeed his servants transform/disguise themselves as servants of righteousness whose end shall be according to their works (actions). 2 Cor 11:14-15**

There is a common thread to all of Satan's scheming and attacks on humanity. Satan wants to take over God's Creation and His authority. He has turned a third of the angels in Heaven against God (Rev 12:4) and now wishes to keep as many of God's children on Earth as possible from listening to Him. The truth of the matter is that whoever is not listening to God, is in reality listening to Satan (John 8:42-47 and more).

If Satan can keep people focusing on themselves and their families, in reality, he has kept them from knowing God and His love for all. If people start listening to God, some will start obediently interacting with Him, and God will develop within them a loving trust for Him due to His love and faithfulness. Those who choose to listen to God and obey Him will eventually come to a place in their lives of turning from self to God and His way of life (repentance) and experience spiritual birth into His eternal holy family.

Journeying with Others toward Destruction

In his battle for ultimate control over everything, Satan has been constantly trying to preoccupy humanity with itself, scare humanity into submission, and/or turn humanity from God through the introduction of many counterfeit gods and religious institutions. Some of these counterfeits scare people into submission and others encourage people to remain self-centered living predominately for themselves and their families.

In order to keep people focused on themselves instead of properly considering others, Satan has filled our world with counterfeits to replace God. Because Satan cannot remove knowledge of our Creator from humanity, he has created a myriad of religious institutions to confuse and/or placate many. In reality, through deceptions and half- truths, these false gods and hurtful philosophies satisfy many and help keep them away from the one true Creator. The last thing that Satan wants is for people to know reality.[135] In addition to riches, personal aspirations, entertainment, and even laziness, Satan uses individuals and fabricated religions to distort reality making it harder for people to know their one true Creator. Even with all of Satan's cunning deceptions, he cannot completely disguise his deceptive false teachings because they *all* exhibit some of his personal attributes, some much more than others. The better that you come to know God and His Word, the easier it is to recognize Satan and his counterfeits.

Self-centeredness

If Satan can keep people thinking about themselves as the center of life, he has won. Due to the sin of God's first created, Adam and Eve, all are born into a self-centered, selfish world that is in constant rebellion against God and His standards (Rom 5:6-10). Satan uses the desires of fallen humanity against itself. If an individual is focused primarily on himself or herself, Satan is quick to remove anything that these individuals may have heard that is true about God from the forefront of their thoughts and replace that with substitutes (Matt 13:19).

Loss of the Familiar

As the Holy Spirit leads and individuals start thinking about God, Satan will try hard to make their lives miserable through many circumstances including the loss of friends and

---

[135] 2 Cor 4:3-4; cf. John 8:44.

outbursts of others in the world. Satan knows that most people like what is familiar and will not move easily into unfamiliar realms to include friendships without a good reason (Matt 13:20-21). But as God encourages all and some start trusting Him even a little, He is faithful to continue to draw them to Himself. He will teach them a better way of life based on a genuine love/concern for all.

Worldly Success

When one considers following Jesus, he or she may encounter an even greater hurdle than making new friends. Jesus will start to reshape their priorities including redefining success, which may move Satan to tempt them with additional income. If he is able to keep them distracted with additional resources that require additional time, many will lose their developing spiritual connection to God and go back to following other gods including money (Matt 13:22).

Following Jesus and Intensifying Battles

For those who start following Jesus wanting to live their lives according to our Heavenly Fathers' will and ways, the battles normally intensify. Satan will continue to battle against them trying to reduce their witness to the world through various forms of distraction. Satan knows that if he can distract Jesus' followers through some form of busyness or intimidation, they will not do God's assigned good works well, which in turn helps keep non-Christians in the dark and away from God. Therefore, Jesus' followers need to stay focused and intentionally journeying with God doing His good works. They should keep in mind that they are the light of the world and that God works through them, not around them. They are the physical hands and feet of Jesus.

In my own life, I have had many times when I became aware of God's desire for me to do some task that would help His kingdom work both physically and spiritually. Many times without fail all types of situations would come up to distract me from doing my assignments (Matt 6:25-33). As I look back over more than forty years of following Jesus as an adult, I pray that I have completed God's desired purposes for me at least twenty percent of the time. If we do not stay focused on Jesus (Heb 12:1-3) and His will for our lives, it is easy to be sidetracked. I can recount everything from simple emergency repairs on our house or cars, to immediate family needs, to some other ministry needs, or even to expansion of current ministry or work that would try to pull me away from doing a mission that God had placed on my heart. I know that I am not alone in experiencing these types of spiritual attacks.

No Pain, No Gain

Another common deception permeating many of our churches today is the idea that God does not want us to work through anything that is difficult. Many of Jesus' followers are led to believe that if something is difficult, God must be shutting the door on that assignment. ***That is not true!*** Some of Jesus' followers just do not know any better, but there is a second group within our churches who do not know Jesus and therefore have no clue about what it means to deny themselves, pick up their individual crosses, and follow Him (Luke 14:26-27). This group of potential followers of Jesus confuse those who are truly trying to follow Him. Satan uses them to make complacency and other abnormalities look normal (2 Cor 11:14-15).

The norm for a true Christian is ***to be radically different*** than those not listening to God as he or she tries to follow the leading of God. All we have to do is look at the New Testament accounts of our forefathers as they ministered in the first century and realize that most went through many trials and tribulations as they followed Jesus.

Following Jesus is not suppose to be easy, but it should be fulfilling! Following Jesus will not be easy because the battle over the outcome of every single life ***is*** significant. God loves everyone and wants all to come to a place in their lives where they will turn from their self-centered ways to Him and His ways, and in so doing be saved (2 Peter 3:9). We need to always keep in mind that there are eternal consequences for our actions, and that the outcome of faithful discipleship will bring some to a saving relationship with God.

Meaningful Relationships

Satan has caused many to replace meaningful periods of work and social interaction with self-centered entertainment and/or technological activity that helps one feel productive but, in reality, keeps people too preoccupied to develop meaningful relationships. Many are now spending unnecessary long periods each day texting, emailing, internet browsing, gaming, and all sorts of self-absorbing activities that are contrary to building solid godly relationships. This type of activity is one of the new drugs of the twenty-first century. ***Self-centered activity and entertainment are easy. Working hard and building meaningful godly relationships takes time and effort but if worked through normally produces the most fulfilling lives.***

As we come to know God and His desire for our lives, we begin to understand the importance of a close mature holy relationship with God and one another. Even within everyday activities, Satan is at work destroying godly relationships through many perversions of things that God created for good (2 Tim 2:22-26).

Consider food: God has created food to sustain our temporary physical bodies. Satan has caused many to substitute overeating, for godly intimate relationships. Overeating may be easy, building caring intimate relationships normally takes work.

Consider drugs: God has given us the wisdom to use certain drugs and natural supplements to assist the body. Satan has caused many to misuse all types of chemicals and supplements as a substitute for godly caring relationships that serve one another. The misuse of drugs may be the easier way to cope at times, but putting the work into building caring relationships is well worth the work.

Consider sex: God has created sex as one of our bodily functions in order to procreate building family units with the potential of adding to His eternal holy family. It should also help increase intimacy between a man and a woman within a life-long marriage relationship. Yet, Satan has caused many to substitute perverted forms of sex instead of building godly intimate caring relationships. Perverted sex may be temporarily satisfying, but building a godly caring relationship between a man and a woman within the confines of marriage will produce the best and most fulfilling relationship. And keep in mind that a godly marriage is the basis of a sound family structure for the proper edification of our children and in reality is best for the whole human race.

Beware, Satan is out to kill and destroy as many caring relationships as possible. ***If one listens to God,*** solid caring relationships will be built, which bring lasting fulfillment, long lasting joy, and inner peace.

Heaven or Hell?

Have you ever wondered why God does not just take each of us into Heaven and show us around and then take us to Hell and do likewise, so that we might be able to make an informed decision of where we want to live for eternity? At one time in my life, I did. It seemed that manifesting the two worlds would be an easier way to convince many to follow Him. But, as I became more grounded in God's Word, I realized that ***God does not want anyone making a decision to follow Him based on material things but instead on godly eternal interactive relationships.***

Although Heaven is going to be a great place to call home, a place that will make even the most beautiful places on earth seem mediocre, God wants us to base our eternal choice of family and friends on a desire to live with Him and others in a truly caring interactive community versus basing our decision on the physical pleasantries of an environment. If we do not submit to our Heavenly Father due to His great love for everyone and allow Him to complete our transformation into His caring nature toward all, we have automatically chosen Hell for our eternal home.

Hell

When we look to God's Word to understand the living conditions of the Kingdom of Hell more fully, we come away with a deeper desire to help as many as possible make good choices about their relationship with God and man. Hell is a very disturbing and hurtful place. Once one is imprisoned there, he or she stays forever.[136]

We learn from Scripture that those who are placed in Hell undergo eternal shame and suffering. We see metaphorical imagery depicting physical pain compared to being burned continuously by fire and an eternal worm devouring the flesh but never completing the task (Isa 66:24; Mark 9:47-48). We also see the emotional pain of Hell as something similar to having just experienced the loss of a loved one who is very dear to you causing much "weeping and gnashing of teeth [Matt 8:12; 13:42; 25:30]." There are also other metaphorical images of general humiliation, shame, and discomfort including metaphorical imagery of sleeping on a bed of maggots and having a giant worm for a covering (Isa 14:11; Dan 12:2). We do not have explicit statements regarding the shame, pain, suffering, and humiliation of being eternally in Hell, but we have enough metaphorical imagery that shouts loudly, ***"beware, stay out, shame, pain, suffering, and humiliation ahead!"***

Before Jesus died on a cross for the sins of all, Sheol/Hades was the place where ***all*** went when they died, because everyone had to wait for the Messiah's atoning work. Until He came, all waited in either upper or lower Sheol. Upper Sheol contained those who had come to trust and obey God during their lifetime while lower Sheol contained those who had not.

The Old Testament writers knew of a range of depth within Sheol.[137] Jesus' account of Lazarus and the rich man's death and subsequent life in Hades/Sheol helps us understand that there are

---

[136] Dan 12:2; Matt 25:46; cf. Rev 20:11-15.

[137] Deut 32:22; Prov 9:18; and more.

two major areas within Hades with the higher reserved for the faithful and preferred over the second, which was further down in the depths of Hades and reserved for those who had not listened to God and followed His way of life. From Jesus' promise to one of the criminals with whom He was crucified, we learn that he was going to be with Him that very day in the upper area of Hades, which Jesus called "Paradise."

The ungodly group is still presently waiting in lower Sheol (Hades) for the final trial and judgment. At that time, they will stand trial before Jesus, who will be seated on His great white throne, and be sentenced to appropriate punishment according to their actions along with a sentence of eternal isolation from God, which is also known as the second death (Rev 20:11-15).

After Jesus spent three days in Sheol proclaiming the goodness of God, the Father raised Him from the dead, and Jesus raised those who lived in the upper area of Sheol, Paradise, and escorted them into His Father's presence (Eph 4:7-10). Ignatius (A.D. 37-107), an early Christian writer and martyr, said that after dying on a cross, Jesus went down into Hades alone but ascended with a multitude having torn down the "middle-wall," which had been dividing God and man.[138] It appears from Paul's testimony, that after Jesus' resurrection, Paradise (Upper Sheol) was moved into an area of heaven called the "Third Heaven," which God allowed Paul to visit and hear things that encouraged him, but that he dared not repeat (2 Cor 12:1-5).

Those who were trusting God prior to the Cross were made perfectly righteous through Jesus' atoning death and were then allowed to be in God's immediate presence. Now, there is only the lower level of Sheol, which contains those from all time who are waiting on their trial due to their rejection of God and His way of life (Rev 20:11-13-15).

---

[138] Ignatius of Antioch, "To the Trallians," Long Version, Book 2, 2.9.4. This matches Scripture such as Acts 2:27, 31 and Eph 4:8-10.

The New Heaven

> **I heard a great voice coming from the Throne saying, "Behold, the dwelling of the [one true] God is with the [redeemed] people, and He shall dwell with them, and they shall be His people, and He shall wipe away every tear from their eyes, and death shall be no more, nor sorrow, nor weeping, nor suffering shall be any more; the first things have passed." Rev 21:3-4**

What about God's desired relationship with us? We know that God has created us to be part of His eternal mature loving righteous close-knit interactive family, and if we receive Him into our lives as ***both lord and savior***, God's desire becomes reality for us. God has created each of us to be an intimate family member experiencing perfect love, peace, and joy with Him forever.

In Jesus' personal revelation to John for His followers, we take note that in our future New Heaven, our Heavenly Father is ***with*** His children (Rev 21:6; 22:1-2). He does not distance Himself in any way from His children, but instead, He is right in the midst of His family, and each individual who learns to trust the Father and Son will be transformed into the likeness of the Father and Son's very nature (Phil 3:20-21; Rom 8:29).

Part of being like Jesus– ***with similar resurrected bodies*** –means that the miracle of Jesus' death on a cross will become reality for all who learn to trust and obey God from the beginning of time right up to the final judgment. In Heaven, all sin has been removed along with any propensity to sin. Without sin in Heaven, there will be no more unrest, pain, sorrow, and death. God's children will drink from the Water of Life and eat from the Tree of Life abundantly (Rev 21:6; 22:1-2; cf. Rom 8:18-23).

When Jesus prayed the night before He died on the Cross as the Savior of the World, we should take special note of the fact that He stated that ***He was sharing His glory with all who were and would be trusting in Him.*** Through His desire to share His sonship and holy nature with His followers, He was insuring our close-knit holy unity. All who become part of God's holy family are guaranteed perfect godly unity with the Father, the Son, the Holy Spirit, and all other eternal holy family members (John 17:20-23).

In Jesus' resurrected body, we note that Jesus could walk through walls, He could change His appearance, people could touch His body and feel substance, He could eat food, and He could ascend in that body from our physical realm into the very presence of His spiritual Heavenly Father. The capabilities of the resurrected body are awesome working within both the spiritual and physical realms.

All who faithfully follow Jesus will have a similar resurrected body with their own unique personal features. They will have the same abilities to operate in both a physical and spiritual world simultaneously within the New Heaven and on the New Earth.

As socially responsible family members, each will take on their assigned responsibilities and corresponding authority. This is why the New Heaven is going to be so great. Have you ever considered what it would be like to live where everyone loved you to the point that you did not ever have to worry about somebody trying to hurt you spiritually, mentally, or physically?

In addition, we will not be hiding from God or others due to past bad actions (sin) because all of our bad actions have been removed. We will become fully known no longer being afraid of what others might think, and we will joyfully serve one another as we take on our assigned responsibilities. We will all be sinlessly serving one another in perfected unbiased love for all under the lordship of the Father and Son. We will be living in a world where our Heavenly Father and Eldest Brother have saved us from the bondage and corruption of sin in order that we may experience an eternal perfect life of love, joy, and peace with Them and one another.

Heaven is going to be great–not because of how great the physical and spiritual realm will be–but because we will finally be free from sin and able to know God and one another perfectly (1 Cor 13:12). At this point in time, we can only imagine what it will be like to speak in casual meaningful conversations with our Heavenly Father, Jesus Christ, the Holy Spirit, and all who have obediently listened to God over the ages. ***Although it seems too good to be true, those of us who are following Jesus are looking forward to that day when we will actually be able to participate in a close relationship with God and one another.***

For those of you who have not really committed to following Jesus up to this point in your life, I encourage you to journey with me a little further and seriously consider following Jesus. Although many who are not following Jesus know that something is wrong and desire something better, Satan has been deceiving them into thinking that things cannot get better. ***This is a lie!*** God gives everyone multiple chances to turn to Him (spiritual awakenings) and obediently follow Him and His way of life. ***It is God who helps people change for the better, which simultaneously improves life in general.***

Resist Satan

When I consider a good friend and a former pastor of mine, Dr. Mark Corts, I remember that his life was anything but easy. God teaches us through the Apostle Peter to ***resist Satan*** and he will eventually flee (1Peter 5:8-9). Jesus' followers should not flee spiritual battles because they serve the one true God, who is with and in them and able to overcome all enemies.

Mark Corts was a follower of Christ who resisted Satan continuously doing what he knew to be right. He constantly had to deal with spiritual battles within his congregation, and for the last fifteen years of his life, he had to deal with ongoing spiritual battles intensified by physical illness. Mark wrote a book prior to his death entitled *The Truth about Spiritual Warfare: Your Place in the Battle between God and Satan*, which discusses some of his battles and spiritual warfare in general.[139] Because of his steadfast work in proclaiming God's Word and his resolve to do God's will at any cost, he became an effective contemporary role model. It was through Mark's willingness to give of himself and follow Jesus faithfully that I came to a place in my life at twenty eight where I was willing to do likewise and made a genuine commitment as an adult to follow Jesus faithfully.

Under Mark's teaching, various Bible classes, and personal Bible study, Jesus not only became my active big brother looking out for me, but He also became *my lord* and *primary mentor*. As I looked at Jesus' life on earth, I began to get a glimpse of what He had given up in Heaven (Phil 2:5-8) and suffered on earth in order to make a way for everyone's sins to be removed.

As I continued to study Scripture, the Apostle Paul became another mentor teaching me what faithful service looked like. When it was the right time, Jesus revealed Himself to Paul and corrected his understanding of God's plan of salvation.[140] From that point on, Paul was willing to give up his religious prestige and secure life in Judea and endure hardship after hardship following Jesus (2 Cor 11:22-31) in order to proclaim the reality of the righteousness of God and His atoning work through Jesus Christ. Paul sacrificed everything in order to help rescue those who did not know God but were willing to listen to the Good News (Gospel) as he proclaimed it through his actions and words.

Jesus did only good as He walked according to His Father's will, and He suffered greatly. Paul suffered greatly after he started following Jesus. Dr. Corts suffered much as he followed Jesus. In general, all who follow Jesus will be asked to give up some of what they could have had for themselves in this world, suffering loss in order to overcome the schemes of Satan. Everything that God asks of His children helps others to see God's love and

---

[139] C. Mark Corts, *The Truth about Spiritual Warfare: Your Place in the Battle Between God and Satan* (Nashville: Broadman & Holman, 2006).

[140] Acts 9:1-20; 22:1-16; Gal 1:11-17.

compassion for all, which in turn helps some come to their senses and ask Him for help in changing their lives to match His. Everything that God asks His obedient children to do will help others to see that there is a better way of life here-and-now and also for eternity, and Jesus' followers will be refined in the process (godly maturity through sanctification; see Rom 6:22 & others).

I believe that Satan's two most effective forms of combat against Jesus' followers are deception and intimidation. His greatest deception is tricking Jesus' followers into thinking that they are not worthy of witnessing, not able to witness, and/or not needed. In reality, all of Jesus' followers are called to witness, enabled to witness through the empowerment of the Holy Spirit, and worthy of witnessing through Jesus' righteousness working in them.

If you fear witnessing for any reason, ask God to give you discernment and empowerment. He will help you know when and how to witness in all circumstances.

Putting on the Whole Armor of God

God empowers and guides those who are listening to Him. Since the Cross, Jesus personally guides, protects, and empowers His followers through ***the indwelling of the Holy Spirit*** (John 14:16-17; Acts 1:8). Jesus' followers from all Christian denominations need to keep their spiritual armor in good working order, properly fitted, and ***on*** at all times in order to see through Satan's deceptions and move according to God's will. The Father Himself protects them as they follow Jesus through the ongoing spiritual battles. At times, God asks His children to give up their physical lives and come Home helping others to know Him through their ultimate sacrifice.

When Paul used the metaphor of putting on the whole armor of God in Ephesians chapter 6 as a way to be prepared to do spiritual battle against Satan and his accomplices, he wanted Jesus' followers to realize that they need God's help, and ***as long as they walk according to God's will, they have all the protection that they need.*** Like a good soldier putting on each piece of defensive and offensive gear in order to be prepared properly for battle, they will be able to overcome Satan and his schemes.

Look at Paul's list of pieces comprising the spiritual armor that all of Jesus' followers are to wear:

> (1) ***truth***, which metaphorically compares to a soldier's carrying belt for all of his spiritual tools;
> (2) ***righteousness***, which metaphorically compares to a soldier's breastplate protecting vital organs;
> (3) ***faith***, which metaphorically provides a movable shield to be positioned as needed to stop Satan's deadly thrusts;
> (4) ***salvation***, which metaphorically provides a helmet covering their heads so that they do not suffer loss of ability to see, hear, and understand what is happening;
> (5) ***knowledge of the Word of God*** through the teaching of the Holy Spirit and willingness to follow His leading, which empowers each with both an offensive and defensive sword in order to clear the way for truth to be known;
> (6) ***preparedness to proclaim the Gospel of Peace***, which makes them effective witnesses wherever God leads; and
> (7) ***continual prayer*** at all times staying in contact with God through ongoing communication: listening and talking.

Living holy lives and handling the Word of God correctly through the instruction and leading of the Holy Spirit allows Jesus' followers to proclaim the "Good News" effectively and defend themselves against Satan and his deceptive practices.[141]

Even if we live righteously, study God's Word, and follow the leading of the Holy Spirit, a holy life does not mean that we will not someday become a casualty of war. Like Jesus, our Heavenly Father is using our efforts including at times the loss of our physical lives for the ultimate building up of His eternal holy family and kingdom, which is also ***our*** eternal close-knit holy family and kingdom. Just know that God will bring good out of every experience of pain and suffering that His children undergo (Rom 8:28; cf. Col 1:24).

---

[141] Eph 6:10-18; 1 Thess 5:14-22.

Chapter 4
Waking Up Spiritually

Have you ever had a dream in which everything happening within the dream felt so real that you were surprised when you woke up and realized that it had all been a dream? In a very similar way, when someone starts listening to God, he or she starts realizing that there is more to the world around them than meets the eye.[142] God does not allow us to interact directly with the spiritual world that is directly interconnected to our physical world, but He gives us awareness of it. Within our physical world, God encourages all to engage in godly social interaction as we consider choosing eternal good over evil.

Although we are not given the ability to interact directly with the spiritual world around us, those who listen to God are taught to understand that many of the battles that we personally experience are spiritually based and can be won ***only*** through His assistance (Eph 6:10-18). The physical world is affected by the spiritual and visa-versa. In the present, we affect the spiritual world through our actions in this physical world including through our prayers as God and His Heavenly Host defend righteousness in both worlds. For those who listen to God, the reality of a future world that is divided into two isolated regions called Heaven and Hell becomes the main focus even as we live out our physical lives in the here-and-now (1 Peter 1:3-9; 2:9-10). ***Our present world is temporary, and the future sinless Heaven and sinful Hell are permanent.***

From the beginning of the Creation, God has asked everyone to make choices. Originating from Adam and Eve's sin of partaking of the fruit of the tree ***of the knowledge*** of good and evil,

---

[142] Compare Rom 13:11; 1 John 1:5-10; 2:15-29; John 3:19-21.

we are all born into sin and forced to experience both good and evil. We learn from both and then must choose to obey or disobey, to follow God or continue in our self-centered ways. It has been part of God's creative design to give everyone a fairly extreme amount of free will in order to allow each person to decide if he or she wants to join Him and others in a mutual caring interactive righteous way of life. God does not stand over His Creation as a hovering parent forcing everyone to do what is right. Through the Holy Spirit's teaching, God works with our individual consciences and shows us the advantages of living caring righteous gracious (holy) lives with Him.[143]

Although God works righteously and graciously in our lives, many openly rebel against Him and His holy way of life (Rom 5:8-10). Even with open rebellion and sometimes hostility, God persistently works with all not wanting any to perish but all to come to a place in their life where they willingly turn to Him looking for help in living a holy life.[144] As God encourages everyone to know Him and His way of life more fully, many will not change, but others at various levels of rebellion including some hitting rock bottom will start willingly submitting to His authority because they come to realize how good He is and how trustworthy and able He is to complete the good Creation that He has started. They start changing from self-rule to seeking His leadership, which leads to a much better life now and forever.[145]

Today, some think that God loves us so much that He will not allow anyone to reject Him and go to Hell or that going to Hell will be temporary and just feel like an eternity. ***This is wrong!*** Without submission to God out of a growing love, people will eternally be confined in the future to an isolated place, a prison, called the Lake of Burning Fire or more commonly "Hell." ***What one decides while physically living truly matters!***

---

[143] Rom 1:18-32; 2:11-16; and others.

[144] 2 Peter 3:9; cf. 1 Tim 2:4.

[145] John 10:9-11; Rom 6:22; Rev 21:1-4.

Born into Sin

As we consider God's Creation, we can make a few observations:

> (1) everyone was created as an eternal being without having a say in the matter;
> (2) everyone other than Adam and Eve was born into a world corrupted by sin and is living on a common wide life-path (road) leading eventually to eternal shame and pain with marred characters if they do not get off; and
> (3) everyone who learns to trust and obey God out of a growing love for Him will get off the wide-road and start following Jesus as a member of God's eternal close-knit holy family.

So, how marred are we, and why would anyone want to submit to God's lordship? God tells us not to love the fallen corrupted world nor the various ways of the world because they are not of Him.[146] He describes the ways of the world as a life based on self-centeredness versus centered on God and a love for all.

Let's consider a couple uncaring sons within the Prodigal Son parable recorded in Luke 15:11-32. As we look at Jesus' teaching about a loving father and ***two*** self-centered sons (Luke 15:1-2, 11-32), we note three important points:

> (1) the loving father worked hard to provide for his family and workers. From the limited information given within the story, it is noted that He lived his life with a genuine concern for the people around him;
> (2) the openly rebellious younger son was not concerned with others nor the future. When he became old enough to be on his own, he left home living in the moment in such a way as to experience as much worldly pleasure as possible

---

[146] 1 John 2:15; and they will not last 2 Peter 3:7-13; Rev 22:1.

not considering how that would affect his future; and (3) ***the second son,*** who was also highlighted in Jesus' story, demonstrated a certain degree of faithfulness to his father by staying home and helping to maintain their land, but ***he was also distant from God*** because of his lack of genuine love for others shown through his lack of love for his lost brother.

In reality, Jesus' story closes with two lost sons, who have experienced love from their biological father, and who had not yet allowed God to grow genuine love and concern in them. One son came home repenting because of a chance for a better life that his father might offer him, and the other who stayed at home was living legally within his father's moral criteria but did not have a genuine love for others starting with his lost brother.

When Jesus closed this story, He did not say whether either son had a genuine love for their father or others. It is possible that eventually both–having experienced totally different circumstances–would eventually come to the place of allowing God to teach them to love others according to His standards. If they did not, neither would be allowed into God's eternal holy family. Allowing God to lead and teach each of us to love Him and others more and more is crucial to becoming part of His eternal family.[147]

In this story, note that Jesus is talking primarily to the antagonistic Pharisees. The Pharisees are known to be morally good and can be compared to many of our contemporary church members. Many church members today have fairly good morals but are lacking a genuine concern for others. It is a good and noble thing to follow God's moral laws faithfully; but without genuine love and concern for others, one is missing what is most important (1 Cor 13:1-8a).

Jesus makes us vividly aware that the ability to know good and to do good comes only from our Heavenly Father.[148] He is the

---

[147] Matt 5:43-48; 22:37-40; Luke 10:30-37.

[148] Matt 19:17; Luke 18:19; John 20:17.

One who is good, and all goodness flows from Him. Therefore, we need the Creator to help us evaluate our motives for the things that we do. The only way to realize any true godly love is to live out our lives listening to God as we live according to His standards. God wants us to experience a good life and helps all who listen to Him grow in their love for others as He loves all.[149]

During Moses' day, God taught those who would follow Him that they had to live loving-kind righteous (holy) lives: lives that were distinctly separate from those who were not walking in His ways. Israel agreed to follow God and was commanded to be a holy nation manifesting God's true caring nature to the entire world (Ex 19:5-6). They were to be a light to the world just as Christ's followers are today (1 Peter 2:9). From the very beginning, God has wanted as many as are willing from all nations to join Him as part of His eternal holy family. God with His righteous nature does not allow the co-existence of good and evil in His eternal presence knowing that such brings corruption and pain (Rom 8:18-23). That is why Scripture teaches us over and over again that God is holy and demands that we, His created children, strive for holiness (Lev 18:1-5; 19:1-2; and more).

Sin Removal Is a Necessity

Because our Heavenly Father is holy, and it appears that He will not allow sin to exist in close proximity to Him for any real length of time, Paul declared emphatically that "the wages of sin is death (eternal separation from God) [Rom 6:23]!" He also stated emphatically that, "all have sinned and are falling short of the Glory of God [Rom 3:23]." After his encounter with the risen Lord, Paul came to understand that he and many of countrymen had not really understood the necessity of God performing a costly miracle stemming from His righteousness to remove sin from their lives.[150]

---

[149] John 13:34; 15:10-13.

[150] Rom 1:16-17; Phil 3:4-11; Heb 1:2-3; 2 Cor 5:21.

In God's economy, sin, our bad actions, had to be removed like bad cancer cells, not covered up. When we begin to understand how righteous God really is and that we all have some sin in our lives, we can make this personal by joining Isaiah and saying with him, "Woe to me, because I have been cutoff (from God) because I am a man of unclean lips . . . (I know this because) my eyes have seen the King, Yahweh, (who is leader) of the (Heavenly) Hosts (who is holy, holy, holy) [Isa 6:5; see also 6:3]."

Well, as we begin to understand why God does not allow anyone with any sin in His eternal family (Rom 8:18-23 & more), we begin to understand that we have a real problem. We begin to understand that God is holy and that ***sin is unacceptable over a long period of time! It is like cancer. If unchecked it will destroy godly relationships with God and one another.*** Yet, we know that God has created us to be with Him in close proximity as close-knit holy family members. In addition, we realize that although God gave us the written Law through Moses as one of His many acts of grace, neither the Law nor our obedience to His laws have saved anyone because of ***everyone's failure*** to live out the requirements of the Law perfectly.

To live in God's immediate presence for eternity, there must be ***no sin*** with its resulting harm to relationships and the world in general. ***We come face-to-face with the reality that without God's help, we would all face the second death spoken of in Revelation 20:11-15***. We would not have the victory through Jesus over sin and death that Paul was celebrating in 1 Corinthians 15, when he declared, ***"O Death, where is your victory! [15:55-56]"***

Becoming Sinless (Justification)

As we reflect on our Heavenly Father's supreme righteous act of love on our behalf, the death of His Son Jesus, the prophesied Messiah, we come to realize that although the Father suffered great agony over His Son's rejection and death, both knew that they were making ***the only way possible*** for us to be reconciled to them forever. ***Jesus' death was necessary*** to remove all sin from those who learned to trust Him.[151] In God's economy, the penalty for transgressing others had to be satisfied in such a way that all sin is removed and eternally eradicated. If any of God's Creation was going to live closely with Him for eternity, ***justification, being made righteous without sin, was required; it was not optional.***

When someone becomes aware of God's holiness and his or her own sinfulness, there may be a personal desire to clean up one's life prior to submitting to God and His way of life. The problem is that without God's help, no one is able through his or her own strength to achieve ***perfect*** holiness.

That is why our Heavenly Father made plans prior to implementing the physical Creation to provide a way to remove our sins and renew our character according to His holy nature. It is God's righteous work–not our own–that ultimately has the ability to transform us into loving righteous (holy) beings suitable to live with Him and one another in His Heavenly Kingdom (Rom 1:16-17; Eph 2:8). Through the miracle of Jesus' death on the Cross, those who obediently follow Him have ***all sin removed and are given God's righteousness in exchange*** (2 Cor 5:17, 21; 1 Peter 2:24).

Over the years, I have personally seen many continually reject God's invitation into His holy family, because they wanted to wait until they had their lives more in alignment with His or simply wanted more time to enjoy life on their own terms. No one is able to straighten out his or her life enough to approach God without God's help, and the Good News is that no one has to. God just wants us to come to the place of starting to return His love and desiring to live holy lives thus making a commitment to follow Him. He does the rest. ***It is God who shapes and empowers us so that we may start living godly lives in the here-and-now.***

With this in mind, let us consider again the meaning of reconciled sonship as described in Romans 8:28-30. Our Heavenly Father is telling us that ***if we learn to love Him*** because of His great love for us:

> (1) we are ***called*** (***chosen***) and He will help us to mature more and more into the likeness of Jesus with His great grace and righteousness;

---

[151] John 3:14-15; Greek *dei*, "it is necessary."

(2) we are ***justified:*** our sins are removed through a great miraculous work of God through Jesus' atoning death on a cross and time spent in Sheol/Hades, who personally made our bad actions (sins) His, and in exchange for our sins, He has given us some of His righteousness;[152] and
(3) we are ***glorified***, given full-sonship and eventual perfect moral character matching Jesus' sonship and character.

As we learn to start trusting and obeying Jesus out of a growing love, we begin to stand upon our Father's promises. As we start walking with God, we start to develop a trust for His perfect plan for an eternal holy family and corresponding peace and begin looking forward to the day that we will be in Heaven with Him. As we join God in His Great Work of Love, His Creation, and allow Him to develop us over time, we come to realize that we will not reach perfection during this portion of our eternal life, but ***we trust God to complete our transformation*** (Heb 1:2-3). As the Father continually softens our hearts and strengthens our resolve to follow Jesus more fully, we become more and more compassionate toward others. There is great comfort in knowing that in the not-to-distant future, we will have our sins totally removed and will be conformed perfectly into Christ's moral nature as we enter God's immediate presence where there will be no more pain nor sorrow.

Choices Have Consequences

God created everyone with abundant free will requiring each person to make decisions that have eternal consequences and does not force Himself or His way of life on anyone. It is clear from Scripture that God would like everyone to learn to trust Him and choose to live with Him for eternity (John 8:51; 11:25-26 & more), but He knows that many will want to live life their own way and reject His leadership. He consistently encourages everyone to look beyond themselves and choose a life of unbiased love, peace, and joy with Him and others who want the same thing.

---

[152] Rom 3:21-28; Gal 3:13-14; Col 2:13-14; 2 Cor 5:21; 1 Peter 2:24.

With abundant free will being a critical element of God's Creation, it is also clear from Scripture that God gives everyone multiples opportunities (spiritual awakenings) to learn to trust and obey Him. When the Creation is finalized, our Heavenly Father, Jesus, and the Holy Spirit want the members of Their close loving righteous family to interact maturely and freely within the Family under the overall leadership of the Father.[153]

Although the first individuals of God's Creation, Adam and Eve, went against Him and His commandment that instructed them not to partake of the fruit of the tree of knowledge of good and evil (Gen 2:16-17; 3:1-6), we would all have done the same due to the lure of knowing and experiencing the unknown, if we thought that we might come out better in the long run through the experience.

What Adam and Eve did not know is that this disobedient act would cause much pain and sorrow for them and all of their descendants, but God knew ahead of time what they would do, what everyone else would do throughout the Creation, and what They would do to create a free-will ***sinless*** eternal family.

Although God knew in advance that all of His Creation would struggle because of Adam and Eve's decision to disobey Him, He placed such a high value on creating everyone with the ability to make important eternal decisions that He allowed such and provided a way to restore fully those who learned to listen to Him. All of this was done so that God's Creation would come to completion with a ***volunteer*** eternal close-knit sinless family that would live together in mutual love, peace, and great joy in a spiritual-physical state that matches Jesus' resurrected state (Phil 3:20-21).

With our great freedom to make choices comes great personal responsibility. It is important to remember that in order to become a mature loving-kind righteous sinless child of God, we must play by His rules following His righteous ways.[154] There are some today who think that God's ways are antiquated, and

---

[153] 1 Cor 11:3; 15:28; cf. Eph 1:15-23; Heb 1.

[154] Lev 19:2; Matt 25:46; 1 John 2:29; 3:10; cf. John 8:51.

therefore, we can reject those portions of His life instructions (commandments) that we do not like.[155] ***This is false! Keep in mind that all of God's ways are based on His eternal nature*** and are for everyone's good. We should continuously thank God for His patience in teaching us how to live holy lives giving those who listen the best life possible now and forever.

Through His parable about a wedding feast, Jesus warns everyone including religious leaders that God judges all according to their heart and actions. All are called at various times, but only those who come in proper attire are allowed to stay (Matt 22:1-14). He concluded this parable by warning those listening that "many are called (invited), but few chosen."

As individuals begin to ask God for help, some start to understand reality more fully through the teaching of the Holy Spirit. This helps them to see more fully the good and bad existing in the world, which in turn brings some to a place of wanting God's help to live according to His way of life,[156] which includes following Jesus (Luke 14:26-33). Within the process of receiving God into their lives and learning to love and trust Him, the moment that they truly want Him to be lord as well as savior turning from self to God and His way of life, God gives them spiritual birth into His eternal holy family.[157]

Jesus taught that even some of those who called Him "lord" would not be in Heaven because they were not striving to do the will of His Father (Matt 7:21), and therefore, in reality, they did not have a relationship with Him (Matt 7:23). He followed this teaching with a parable that taught the importance of having a strong foundation for life, which is God and His way of life. If we want a life with lasting love, joy, and inner peace, our foundation for life needs to be God and His way of life (Matt 7:24-27). This is why Jesus warns everyone that if they are not willing to listen to Him

---

[155] Isa 40:8; Matt 5:17-20; Luke16:17.

[156] John 4:34; 8:31b-32.

[157] John 1:11-13; Rev 3:20; Eph 1:13-14.

they are not worthy to be His followers (Luke 14:27). Everyone who desires to be a member of God's eternal holy family must willingly follow His leadership (Luke 14:26).

In reality, there are no "do overs." The writer of Hebrews said that it is appointed for each of us to *die once* and then *a judgment* (Heb 9:27). ***There is no reincarnation!*** All people live this physical portion of their eternal life *only one time*, and all will be judged according to the way that they responded to God during this short portion of eternity (1 Peter 1:17).

Although it may be hard to believe, the hardest part of life for most people is ***just waking up*** to the reality of the spiritual world around them. If we do not listen to God and allow Him to teach us, ***our personal desires remain similar to little children's and they cloud our reasoning*** blinding us to what is really going on (rationalization).

Our self-centered desires along with Satan's deceptions and busyness combine to produce a mental and spiritual smokescreen keeping many from coming to know God well. At times, God breaks through that smokescreen and reveals Himself. ***Through His revelation***, we come to realize how empty our lives are without a close relationship with Him and that He has many faithful followers working worldwide bringing as many as will listen into His eternal presence.

God brings bits of reality into all people's lives through personal revelation, evangelists, preachers, teachers, family members, friends, associates, and even strangers. In our modern world, there are many ways to disburse information including pamphlets, magazines, books, phones, computers, ipads, android tablets, radio, TV, and more. Through these various forms of media, God asks us all to study and reflect on His written Word, the Bible, in order to dispel the darkness around us. This helps us see reality more clearly freeing us more and more from the bondage of sin.[158]

Billy Graham once wrote about a young lady who had written him a letter telling him how totally miserable she had been

---

[158] John 8:31-34; cf. John 8:51; 11:25-26.

in her former free-spirited life. She had been pursuing the sensual pleasures of this world but found neither inner peace nor lasting joy from such. Through God's guidance, she decided to go to a Bible study and stump everyone with her cynicism. Instead, God used that time to build an interest in her to read His Word. She began studying His Word on a regular basis and several months later God brought her to a point where she realized that He really loved her and had a much better plan for her life than she had for herself. At that point, she submitted her life to her loving Creator. She said in her letter that after committing to follow Jesus, she experienced a happiness that she did not know existed. She stated that all those sensual pleasures were traps that had led her to confusion, unhappiness, guilt, and near-suicide. Now she was truly free as she followed Jesus.[159]

One of my former seminary students, Dr. Greg Viehman, tells through his book, *The God Diagnosis*, about some of his spiritual awakening moments where God eventually got through to him by having him consider the potential outcome of his life if it were not eternal. After his death, would he, his family, and all of their memories just become like the shifting sand of a sea with no remaining evidence of the lives they had lived? [160]

Later, after Greg's two sons experienced sadness due to the Christian neighborhoods' children not allowing them to join them while playing (pp. 34-35), Greg started studying the Bible so that he might prove to his Christian neighbors that they were not properly following God's loving righteous way of life. While studying God's Word, God helped Greg focus on three questions: (1) why couldn't Jesus give everyone eternal life if He was God; (2) if Jesus was God, why was He crucified; and (3) why didn't God create many ways to Heaven instead of only one (p. 43)?

---

[159] Billy Graham, *How To Be Born Again* (Waco: Word Books, 1977), 152-53.

[160] Greg E. Viehman, M.D., *The God Diagnosis: a Physician's Shocking Journey to Life after Death* (Sylacauga, AL: Big Mac Publishers, 2010), 11-15.

After a fair amount of investigation into the Word of God including proving its historical accuracy, Greg came to the point of intellectually accepting the Apostle John's eyewitness account of Jesus and His atoning work (p. 108). He was now ready for God to give him a final spiritual awakening, a personal review of his sins and the opportunity to ask God for forgiveness of those sins (pp. 116-119, 192).

After Greg received Jesus into his life as lord and savior, he was born spiritually into God's family and felt like he had just awakened from a thirty-six year dream, a dream based on deception (pp. 121, 181). Now that Greg was malleable as a new creation in Christ, God started molding him into His moral image (sanctification). Soon after being born spiritually and realizing that he was changing, Greg started self-diagnosing and came to realize that through the work of the Holy Spirit, his personality was becoming more like Jesus' and his spiritual understanding was improving dramatically (pp. 166-168).

God Is Always at Work

Part of the Good News (Gospel) is that God is always at work helping as many as will listen understand the reality of the physical and spiritual realms of this world (John 5:17; 18:37). ***Everyone senses both realms*** through what they see in the physical world and what the Holy Spirit helps them see spiritually,[161] but keep in mind that it is only through their willingness to listen to the Creator that anyone is able to understand some of what is really going on around them.[162] Through God's help, everyone has the potential to understand something of both realms.

It is sad that for most, God has to allow bad things to happen in order to get people's attention. It seems that when things are going well according to our way of thinking, we do not have

---

[161] Rom 1:18-22; 2:11-16; John 3:19-20.

[162] John 3:21; 7:17; Acts 22:14a; 1 Cor 2:10, 16.

the time nor desire to listen to God even when we are not experiencing the type of full life that He desires for us. Yet, God remains persistent working with all to awaken those who are willing to listen. The Holy Spirit is always actively working in everyone's heart and mind. Sometimes God gets our attention during quiet moments, sometimes through miraculous events, sometimes through tragedies including near death experiences, and in many cases through everyday experiences.

The greatest spiritual battle that every individual has to face is whether he or she will allow God to awaken him or her from the dreamlike state in which he or she lives. In reality, it normally feels safer and more comfortable to stay in this dreamlike state than to wake up. This state is somewhat like an altered state of consciousness wherein each individual has found a familiar place within a certain group of friends and activities to avoid the unknown whether good or bad.

Allowing God to awaken us to the reality of the existing spiritual realm that permeates and influences our physical world can be just as traumatic as getting off drugs. God consistently works with us to awaken us to the reality of our spiritual and physical world and the consequences of our ongoing decisions.

For those who listen, God starts them on a path within a much bigger world than first realized. Those who allow God to awaken them start realizing a need to reevaluate past presuppositions and make appropriate adjustments in order to realize a proper relationship with God and others. Their understanding of their world starts shifting from one that had been very self-centered to one that becomes more and more in tune with God, His standards, and His Creation. God is bringing as many as will listen into alignment with His holy nature producing eternal lives full of love, joy, inner peace, and excitement.

For all who allow God to awaken them from their personal self-centered worlds and start learning to trust and obey the Creator of the universe, they eventually come to realize that:

> (1) life is truly eternal for all people of all time with good or bad eternal consequences depending on choices made during each person's physical life;

(2) those who obediently listen to God immediately become part of His eternal close-knit holy family and are given "good work"[163] assignments during their physical lives; and (3) those who obediently listen to God will eventually be fully transformed into Jesus' perfect moral nature and live forever with Them and the rest of Their close-knit holy family members in Heaven experiencing continuous ongoing godly love, joy, and inner peace.

Coming to Our Senses: Spiritual Awakening

. . . there was a great famine . . . and he desired to eat his fill . . . and coming to himself (his senses) . . . and arising, he went to his father.
Luke 15:14-20

Have you ever sensed that God has been or presently is saying to you, "Join Me"? God is constantly asking people and nations to wake up, understand the consequences of sin, and begin living holy lives with Him. In Jesus' day–as in every period of history–many people stayed busy building their careers and estates. But, too much busyness is counterproductive in developing relationships with the Creator and others. Whether it is technological distractions, general entertainment, perversions, perverted relationships, work, or just busyness in general, one should not allow busyness to sidetrack one from listening to God. Through the Holy Spirit's work and Jesus' leadership, the Father uses His faithful people of every generation to help awaken those who are spiritually slumbering through personal interaction. He also uses personal crises and other events in the life of each person to either draw people to Him or strengthen those who are already committed and following Him.

Initially, most people do not listen to God. Instead, many ask some of Satan's counterfeit gods to help them fulfill their

---

[163] Eph 2:10.

desires and needs or they simply count solely on their own ability. Just as this is true today including counting on the many gods of resources or success, this was true thousands of years ago.

Even today many people, who proclaim that there is only one true God, consider Him more like a genie who might help them with various difficulties in life, instead of seeking His help in building a sound personal relationships with Him. But, the Good News includes the fact that God is at work with all encouraging as many as will listen learn to care about Him, His ways, and other people outside their families.

For those who start to listen beyond their immediate concerns, God starts guiding them off the wide-road leading to separation from Him and onto their individualized tailored roads with Him. These individualized narrow roads comprise the biblical narrow road that leads through Jesus into eternal life with God. In addition, this narrow road leads those who listen into the good works that the Father has assigned (Eph 2:10 and more).

In addition to what God teaches everyone about Himself through His Creation, He asks all who are willing–whether committed to Him yet or not–to learn more about Him through the reading of His Word.[164] God has inspired each of the writers of the Bible, and it profits all who read and then act appropriately to what they have read (2 Tim 3:16-17). The Holy Spirit will teach ***those who have a genuine desire to do what God desires*** (John 7:17).

Keep in mind that everyone starts out with some level of blindness not fully seeing the devastating consequences of their bad actions, but to help overcome this blindness, ***God gives everyone moments of awakening with its corresponding lucidity.*** During those lucid moments, everyone has to go through an inner struggle deciding whether or not they are willing to give up some of their temporary worldly pleasures. It is during these lucid moments that individuals realize that God has a better life for them, if they are willing to follow Him and His way of life versus their own ways. But many stay focused on themselves and soon

---

[164] Deut 4:1; 30:15-16; Ps 103:17-18; 119:5-12.

revert back to the old familiar less satisfying life and remain self-absorbed forgetting the better life that God had just shown them.[165]

But, for those who listen, they become followers of Jesus and is so doing become new creations, who are transformed into God's nature (2 Cor 5:17; Gal 5:22-23). They go through a process learning to love others as God loves all. When they die physically, ***they do not need a pass into Heaven*** from anyone–including church leaders– because they are God's children. They know that Heaven belongs to God ***and*** all of His holy children. They also know that when they die physically, Jesus will meet them as their spirit leaves their bodies, and He will escort them into the presence of their eternal Father.[166]

Is the Cost of Following Jesus Too High?

It is difficult for many people, who are contemplating following Jesus, to start this journey, because they know that one must put aside some personal desires (dying to self) in order to start building a close relationship with God and others. God is asking everyone to set aside some personal pleasure and ambition and accept His individualized path for each (the narrow road).

What I have found over time is that many have difficulty in giving up present personal desires for a life of ongoing service in God's holy family even if that service leads to a more fulfilling life now and an eternally close life with God and others in the future. For many, it just seems really hard to accept such an offer from God because of ***the possible lack of immediate gain***. Even when they know that Heaven is secured by God due to His great ability and power over everything, many still want things their own way. They are not willing to allow God to reshape their character to become more and more like His nor wait for the finalized New Heaven and New Earth without its sin, tears, and sorrow. In reality,

---

165 James 1:23-24; Rev 3:15-20.

166 John 14:3; 1 John 3:1-2; Rev 21:3.

many consider a present life of following Jesus ***too high a cost*** to give up present short-lived worldly pleasures and ambitions even if they could obtain more joy and inner peace now and a perfected eternal life after physical death.

Jesus asks all to consider carefully the cost of following Him in order that no one start out on a journey that they are not taking seriously. He tells all who are considering following Him that they need to put aside personal ambition, commit their lives to helping others know God, and follow His lead within a loving righteous (holy) lifestyle that will include some sacrifice. He warns all that if they are not willing to do such, they will not be able to become part of His eternal holy family that prioritizes love (care) for all over everything (Luke 14:26-33).

Personal investment of time, energy, and resources into the lives of others is part of God's plan for all. In order to successfully implementing God's plan, one must listen to Him and learn to love Him and others (1 Cor 13:4-7). Returning God's love is contingent on getting to know and trust Him. Trust in God is developed through obediently following Jesus and actively stepping out in a growing trust to accomplish His will (Heb 5:14; cf. James 1:22-25).

God is pleased with any and all good that we do, but He is also clear that any sin in our lives that is not removed will prevent us from spending eternity with Him, and He reminds us that all have sinned. At first glance, this sounds pretty bleak, but we should keep in mind that God has created all of us to be with Him forever. So, in reality, He values our choices and wants us to come to a place in our lives that ***we actually want to be with Him not for the things that He can do for us as if He were some uncaring distant genie but because of who He is***. God truly loves and cares deeply about everyone, saved and unsaved, encouraging our godly development and always doing what is best for each.

A Personal Testimony

As we start maturing, most of us find that life is more complicated than what we had been told as a child. By my mid-twenties, I had finished my military duty, undergraduate studies, and was starting a business. In addition, my wife and I had our first child on the way. I had worked hard and was now ready to settle down taking care of my family, continuing to work hard, going to church on Sunday, and seeking occasional times to relax with family and friends.

But, something started to happen along my life journey that probably happens to most people as they live out their adult lives. God persistently and consistently helped me to understand more accurately the finalized world that He is in the process of creating. As I studied His Word and applied what He was teaching me, He helped me understand more fully His eternal plans for a perfect Heaven and a place of separation, a prison, normally called Hell or the Lake of Fire.

I came to realize that being sentenced eternally to Hell was not solely God's judgment for bad behavior but also an alternative life for those who did not want to follow His lordship nor His holy way of life, which is based on a pure impartial love for all. I become more and more aware of God's goodness and came to understand that even prior to the beginning of the physical Creation, God had already made a way for everyone who would live during the Creation to be with Him in His completed perfect world, if they would become willing to return His love and follow His way of life.

As I began to understand God's way of life more fully and understand how good it is to follow Jesus, I started to want to please Him more, and I started letting go of my childhood dreams and receive His much more fulfilling plans for my eternal life.

I do not think that our initial childhood dreams and careers make much difference ultimately in deciding whether or not God is worthy to follow. Some of us may start off without any real aspirations but simply desire to take care of ourselves and our families, while others may have high expectations of rewarding careers in an assortment of fields. Others may simply not care to engage in anything and may just start off drifting without any real direction. But, in all cases whether or not we have followed the One True God from childhood, I believe there comes a time when each of us realizes that there is a living interactive power higher than ourselves and that something is missing in our lives, if we are not interacting positively with that higher power. This is because at various times, God interacts with everyone from every cultural and religious background from conception to physical death encouraging every heart and mind to follow Him and His way of life (spiritual awakenings).[167]

For me after military service, undergraduate college, and within five to six years of successfully growing a company, I started to realize that success and a reasonable amount of money were not as personally satisfying as I had initially thought. While I had been developing our new company, God had been developing me. I was becoming more and more concerned about others through regular exposure to His Word and Jesus' leading through the Holy Spirit. They encouraged me to minister to others including the homeless and those in prison. I started to realize that caring relationships with God and others was the only thing of eternal value.

As I listened to God, He developed within me a love for others that brought me great joy whenever I could help anyone grow in their relationship with Him. I realized that having a right relationship with God was the most important thing that anyone could have now and forever. As I personally grew in my relationship with God, I realized that He was inviting me to limit my business activity and minister more to others. He was asking me to let go of my childhood dreams and accept the good works that He had planned out specifically for me before the physical Creation started. I just needed to follow His lead.

Although I had recommitted my life to following Jesus more closely at twenty-eight, it was not until I reached thirty-seven that I was ready to close my business and take the next step in following Him. Over the following years, I have come to realize that following Jesus is a journey that provides constant godly growth as we learn to trust and obey Him more faithfully day by day–many times in the face of adversity even from those around us.

---

[167] Rom 2:11-16; cf. Rom 1:18-32.

Doing the Will of God

Jesus said that only those who had a desire ***to do the will of the Father*** would come to know Him.[168] He also said that there would be some who called Him "lord" who would not be with Him in Heaven because ***they had not done the Father's will*** (Matt 7:21). If someone wants to know God, he or she must be willing to follow His lead. God does not weigh people's good and bad activities throughout their lives to see if they have done enough good to enter Heaven. In reality, the Father only accepts people into His eternal holy family who are willing to allow Him to shape them into Jesus' moral nature and obediently follow Him. ***God requires commitment with corresponding action (John 3:36; 8:51; Rom 2:13)!***

Just as in Malachi's time, God wants us to trust Him enough to do our part in supporting His creative work. It is one thing to know about something, ***it is something else to love God and others enough to get involved.*** God asks all to listen to Him, learn to return His love, and to step out in faith and do His will. ***Our Creator is seeking out and working with all who love and honor Him through their actions as well as their words*** (Matt 25:31-46; Luke 6:46; Rev 22:12). Let's all be willing to follow Jesus faithfully.

Let's keep in mind that ***now*** is the time for the followers of Jesus of this generation to engage our culture and dispel the spiritual darkness around us. ***Now*** is the time for the Church to demonstrate clearly God's love for ***all*** through our actions as well as our words. Through our spiritual rebirth and faithfully following Jesus, we should experience more and more excitement, joy, and inner peace as we make God more fully known to the world around us.

---

[168] John 7:17; 8:39-47; cf. Matt 25:31-46; Rom 2:13.

There Are No Passes to Heaven

Jesus' followers have not picked up passes to Heaven and are just waiting to go home, and they are not presently sitting on the sidelines acting as spectators watching God at work! Jesus' followers enjoy being interactive co-laborers with the Creator. ***They have the privilege, honor, and duty of representing God on earth*** helping fellow disciples and helping those who are living under the deceptions and leadership of Satan. It brings Jesus' followers ***great joy*** to help fellow followers of Jesus and even greater joy to help rescue those who are not following Jesus from present ungodly lifestyles and future eternal shame, unrest, and suffering.

As part of the universal Church, Paul teaches that Jesus' followers are "in Christ." ***Being "in Christ," means having a close obedient interactive relationship with Jesus, God's Anointed One, the true Messiah. It is critically important to have a close relationship with Jesus in order to function well in the spiritual warfare that is constantly going on around us.*** It is our obedient close association with Jesus that gives us access to the Father and enables us to overcome evil as we train some and lead others to Him.[169] As we faithfully follow Jesus, we come to know more fully the Father's will.

Being "in Christ" is the only way that anyone finds true peace as they are developed more and more by the Father to have the mind of Christ (1 Cor 2:16). Through Jesus' leading through the Holy Spirit, the Father rearranges Jesus' followers' priorities, and they experience great joy being part of His great rescue operation throughout the Creation. Jesus' followers take the necessary time *to make and train* new disciples.

Those who are "in Christ" are also part of the Body of Christ. Jesus is the head of the Body, the Church (Col 1:18). The phrase "Body of Christ" appears in the New Testament to represent Jesus' literal body or figuratively to represent His followers

---

[169] Eph 2:18; 6:10-20.

working together as ***His bodily representatives*** throughout the last part of the Creation following Jesus' resurrection.

Considering the Body of Christ, Paul wants all of Jesus' followers to understand the importance of each member. ***Everyone is important and has work to do under the headship of Jesus.*** When considering any physical living body, each member–whether foot, hand, ear, eye, heart, lungs, kidneys, and the list goes on–has an important contributing function to the overall ability and well being of that body (1 Cor 12:12-25).

Considering how the various members of a living physical body work together for the good of the whole, Paul stressed the importance of ***godly unity*** among the various members of the Body of Christ. In Ephesians, Paul emphasized the importance for Gentile and Jewish Christians to treat each other as ***equal family members*** disregarding the prejudices that they had learned through their various religious and cultural backgrounds (Eph 2:11-22). Paul went on to explicitly state that both Judean (Jewish) and Gentile *Christians* were members of the same family, God's household, which made them family members and fellow citizens of His eternal kingdom. He closed this important teaching on Christian unity by using one last image. Jesus' followers could consider themselves metaphorically as individual parts of the great House of God, which is continually under construction until the last person is added (Eph 2:20-22). Through Jesus, the holy family of God can now experience inner peace within itself despite the various backgrounds, trials, and tribulations of its members.

Chapter 5
Being a Child of God

I do not ask only for these (my immediate disciples), but also for those who will believe in me through their word, that all of them may be one, as you, Father, are in me, and I am in you, that they also may be in us. John 17:20-21a

When Jesus prayed that all people of all time who are believing (trusting) in Him may be "one," united with God and each other, He illuminates the meaning of eternal life and salvation declared in John 3:14-17. Jesus is praying for all who learn to trust and obey Him out of love to be united in the same special way to the Father that He is united to Him.

Because of God's unconditional love for us, we can learn to trust and obey Him. When we examine one of our best known scriptures regarding God's love for us, John 3:16, we see that eternal life is provided for all who ***are believing (trusting)*** in Jesus. The original Greek root *pistis* normally translated as "faith or belief" also has a basic meaning of "trust." This Greek wording is used in verses such as John 3:16 (believing) and Eph 2:8 (faith) in which God declares our salvation through our trust in Jesus.[170] This asserts that our salvation and transformation come through Jesus when we believe in Him and make a conscious decision to trust His faithfulness toward us.[171]

---

[170] In addition, see Rom 1:15-16-32.

[171] Rom 3:22-28; 10:9-13.

As we learn to return God's love through ***interaction*** with Him and others, we gain ***experience*** in trusting God,[172] and it is ultimately through our growing trust that we come to know how and why we exist. Godly faith (trust) is not blind faith; we learn to trust God by entering into His work and experiencing His love and faithfulness toward us in action (Heb 5:13-14). As we walk with God learning to trust Him, we also learn to obey Him because of His great love for us. We develop wanting to please Him.

The apostle John uses the term "Believer" as an individual who has come to know Jesus as ***both*** savior and lord. The Believer trusts and obeys Him out of love.[173] God puts the two words "trust" and "obedience" together because they work hand-in-hand as shown in one of John the Baptist's statements,

> **The one who is believing in (trusting) the Son has eternal life, but the one who is not obeying the Son will not see (eternal) life, but the judgement of God remains upon him.**
>
> **John 3:36**

This verse clearly indicates that those who trust Jesus also obey Him. Jesus tells us that those who obey Him do it out of love.[174] Those who love the Father, love the One whom He sent to save us.[175] If we truly love Jesus, we will learn to trust and obey Him.[176]

We do not naturally obey someone just because we trust them. Although we may know that an individual is honest and will

---

[172] Rom 10:10; Gal 5:6; cf. Heb 5:13-14; cf. Heb 11.

[173] Regarding obedience, examine John 14: 21, 23; Gal 5:6.

[174] John 14:15, 21, 23-24.

[175] Matt 10:40; Mark 9:37; Luke 9:48; John 8:42; 12:44; cf. John 1:29.

[176] John 14:15, 21, 23-24; Gal 5:6.

do everything that they promise, that does not in and of itself obligate nor encourage us to obey them. Trustworthiness without love is not worthy of obedience. We learn to trust God's motives and actions as we learn how much He loves us; He is righteous and loves us so much that He sent Jesus to die on a cross for us. As we reflect on John 3, we begin to realize that in order to be born from above and start our journey homeward to be with God in Heaven, we must allow Jesus to lead us. From the moment that we decide to allow Jesus to be both our savior and lord forever, we are born from above, born of the Spirit; we become God's reconciled children forever.[177] The Holy Spirit dwells within us helping us to communicate with God in close fellowship for eternity as Jesus leads us in our assigned good works.[178]

Being Created in the Image and Likeness of God

After God had created all of the animals according to their own individual kinds, He created humanity in His own image according to the likeness of His own nature. Scripture proclaims that our Heavenly Father working with His beloved Son and Holy Spirit created a people in Their own image according to Their own likeness.[179] This wording informs us that Adam was created in Their image and likeness referring to the Father, Son, and Holy Spirit.

Just as the Son of God has been granted great free will by our Heavenly Father, humanity was granted great free will. Not being bound by time and knowing that everyone would initially rebel against Him, God still insisted that all go through the pain

---

[177] Born From Above: John 3:3-5; Eph 1:13-14; 1 Peter 1:22-23. Being God's Children: Eph 1:4-5, 13-14; Rom 8:14-17.

[178] Holy Spirit: John 14:16-17; 16:13. Good Works: Eph 2:10; 1 Cor 3:9; 2 Tim 1:8-9; Titus 2:14.

[179] Gen 1:24-27: literally "in the image Us," and in the "likeness of Us"; cf. 3:22; Acts 17:22-34; James 3:9.

and corruption caused by bad choices along with learning to make good choices. The Father and Son knew in advance the cost of this free-will righteous volunteer family and were willing to do what it took to produce it. After much pain and suffering, all will be made right by Them for all who learn to return Their love and follow Their leadership.[180]

Even with so much pain generated throughout the Creation, God considers His Creation with its perfected outcome as exceedingly good. Although the sinful acts of mankind in rebellion against Him produces much pain, it was the only way to bring about an abundantly free-will family. Therefore, as we consider the fact that God knows what He is doing, we should note the importance that God places on our ability to make important choices, good or bad, even with so much pain generated by our bad actions (sin).

Brothers and Sisters

One day when Jesus was teaching about the Kingdom of God, someone came to Him and told Him that His mother and brothers were outside and wanted to speak to Him. This became an opportune time to teach those around Him about the inclusiveness of God's eternal holy family. Jesus asked the one who had made the request on behalf of His biological family, "Who is my mother and who are my brothers?" He then proceeded to answer His own question by stretching out His hand toward His disciples and saying, "Behold, my mother and my brothers! ***For whoever will do the will of my Father in Heaven, he is my brother and sister and mother*** [Matt 12:48-50; cf. Luke 8:19-21]."

With this teaching, Jesus wanted those who were present and all future disciples to reconsider the idea of family. Although our biological families are normally closer than any other earthly relationships, Jesus' followers are in reality closer to God and one another than any earthly biological family relationship. Yes, we all

---

[180] Rom 8:18-23; 2 Cor 5:21; Heb 1:2-3; Rev 21:1-4.

have a God-given responsibility to take care of our immediate family members, but Jesus is teaching all who listen that His Heavenly Father is the head of all and that His followers comprise a very close-knit loving righteous (holy) family that is closer than biological relatives. ***Jesus is so close to each of His followers that whenever someone does something good or bad toward any of them, they are also doing it directly for or against Him.***[181]

The Completed Family of God

The godly unity within God's completed eternal holy family will be far superior to even the best family unity on earth due to our present less than perfect nature that struggles to live in righteousness. Ultimately, God's eternal holy family members will love one another with perfect unbiased love loving God and one another as God loves us. Keep in mind that on earth, there are millions of small family units. This is not so in the New Heaven. The small family units will be gone, and there will be one God (Sustainer) and Father of all and one holy Family. Jesus said that in Heaven there would be no marriages, but instead, the Father's children would be like the angels in this regard.[182] When the Creation is complete, there is no longer a need to reproduce. God's eternal holy family will be complete. The present function of creating additional children for God's eternal sinless family through small family units will cease.

Adoption: Our Legal Status as Sons of God

> **He came unto His own, and His own did not receive Him. *But, as many as did receive Him, He gave to them authority to be children of God*, to those who were believing/trusting in His name.**
> **John 1:11-12**

---

[181] Matt 25:31-46.

[182] Matt 22:30; Luke 20:35-36.

The first point made in this passage from John's Gospel presentation is that the majority of God's Creation–including Israel–rejected Jesus' presence in their lives as both lord and savior. The second point is that ***Jesus officially declared that those who actually receive Him are the legal children of God*** (cf. Rev 3:20).

Paul, a skilled lawyer of God's laws (life instructions), lived in a world of Hebrew, Greek, and Roman culture and thought, and he used similar Greek terminology stating that Jesus' followers have the same legal rights as Jesus Himself. This is an important concept. In the first century Greco-Roman world, if you had legal status as a son through adoption, you had all the legal rights of a biological son.

In his letter to the Romans, Paul stated that Jesus' followers were children of God and ***fellow heirs with Christ***, who eventually would be glorified with Him. They were eagerly waiting for the realization of their adoption as sons[183] and the redemption of their bodies, which is purification from sin (Rom 8:15-17, 23). In his letter to the Galatians, Paul stated that those who are chosen by God are received into His eternal holy family through adoption as sons [Gal 4:4-6]."[184] In Ephesians, Paul stated that prior to the physical implementation of the Creation according to God's loving-kindness, He predestined each of those whom He called to adoption as a son through Jesus Christ (Eph 1:3-6; 2:4-7).[185]

We also learn from Paul that those who are called by God are those who learn to return His love. When discussing Jesus' relationship with His followers, he stated that those who returned God' love would be sanctified, justified, and glorified (Rom 8:28-30).

After His resurrection, Jesus told Mary Magdalen to go to His "brothers" and tell them that He was ascending to His father, who was also their father, and His god (lord and sustainer), who

---

[183] Greek *huiothesia*, meaning "adoption as a son."

[184] Ditto: Greek *huiothesia*, meaning "adoption as a son."

[185] Ditto: Greek *huiothesia*, meaning "adoption as a son."

was also their god (lord and sustainer) (John 20:17). In Heaven, God's children, both male and female, are equal beings having assigned responsibilities and authority dependent on their earthly faithfulness to God; on one level, they are all considered as sons (Matt 5:9; Luke 20:34-36; Rom 8:14, 19; Gal 3:26).

Oneness: Extreme Intimacy with God & One Another

> **And not concerning these alone (immediate disciples) am I asking, but even concerning those *who are and will be trusting in me* through their word/message, in order that all of them *may be "one"*[186] just as you, Father, are *in/with* me and I am *in/with* you, in order that even they may be *in/with* us, with the result that the world may believe that you sent me. And the *glory* that you have given to me, I have given to them in order that they may be "one" just as we are "one": I in them and you in me in order that they may be made complete (perfected) into "one" with the result that the world may know that you sent me and that *you love them just as you love me.*"**
>
> **John 17:20-23**

The night prior to Jesus' crucifixion, He prayed aloud to His Heavenly Father allowing everyone to know that He was asking that His eternal holy brothers and sisters have the same close unity with Him, His Father, and one another that He had always had with His Father. Jesus started this part of His prayer saying, "And not concerning these alone (immediate disciples) am I asking, but even concerning those ***who are and will be trusting*** in me through their word/message [John 17:20]."

---

[186] The Greek word *hen* is being translated into the English "one" for all cases in John 17:20-23.

When Jesus started this portion of His prayer, asking on behalf of all people who learn to trust Him, He is helping us understand that through Their Creation, His requested ***godly unity*** for God's expanded holy family is open for all who learn to trust and listen obediently to Him and the Father.

Jesus continued praying, "in order that all of them may be one just as you, Father, are in/with me and I am in/with you, in order that even they may be in/with us, with the result that the world may believe that you sent me [John 17:21]." When Jesus prayed that all present and future disciples may be "one," a close godly unity,[187] with God and one another, He illuminates what it means to be saved and have eternal life with God. Jesus prayed for all who would learn to trust and obey Him out of love[188] to be united in the same special way to His Heavenly Father that He is.[189]

When we look to God's Word for a better understanding of "oneness/godly unity," we are reminded that God said, "Let us make Adam in our image according to our likeness." The Father, Son, and Holy Spirit's unity is so close that Israel considered their God, which was written in the plural form, "our gods," as "one" entity, one triune God.[190] ***Jesus was praying that all who ever learn to love, trust, and obey God would have the same close unity that He has always had with the Father, which includes God's children being loved by the Father just as He is.***

Jesus Shares His Glory

> **Jesus finished this part of His prayer saying, "And the *glory* that you have given to me, I have given to them in order that they may be "one" *just as we are "one";* I in them and you in me in order that they may be made**

---

[187] Greek: *hen*, "a close unity."

[188] John 14:15, 21, 23.

[189] cf. John 10:30; 17:5.

[190] Hebrew: *eḥad*, "one" entity, one god.

> **complete (perfected) into "one" with the result that the world may know that you sent me and that *you love them just as you love me.*" John 17:22-23**[191]

This passage gives us the clearest meaning of what our finalized relationship will be like with the Father, Son, Holy Spirit, and one another. We come to understand that God's Crown Jewel of the Creation, His eternal holy Family, will have a godly unity based on sharing Jesus' glory, which includes His sinless love. Jesus was filled with great joy as He looked forward to providing total sin removal through His atoning death the next day for all people throughout the entire Creation who learn to trust and obey Them out of a developing love (John 17:13). God's timeless love is clearly portrayed through His creative work at the Cross.

In order to make this godly relationship possible within God's eternal close-knit holy family, Jesus shares His glory with His brothers and sisters. Earlier in this prayer, we learned that Jesus asked that His disciples be protected under His Father's name thereby showing that His followers are ***an intimate part of God's eternal holy family*** (John 17:11b). In addition to this request, Jesus declared a powerful truth to encourage all who were trusting God throughout all time by illuminating the truth of their present and future relationship with God and one another.

As we look at John 17:22, we see ***Jesus sharing His glory*** and thereby making it possible for those who will return God's love to come into His Father's household ***with the same unity that He has always had with His Father.*** The glory that Jesus is sharing with His followers stems from His relationship with the Father and His resulting character. Jesus is like His Father, who is full of grace and truth. As described in John 1:14, Jesus' glory is similar to His Father's glory as described in Exodus 33:18-19 and 34:6. Jesus' nature matches His Father's, who is full of grace and truth. It is Jesus' sonship ***and*** loving righteous character that accentuate His glory and attracts individuals to Him much

---

[191] Greek *hen,* is being translated as "one"; cf. John 14:19-21.

more than His intellect and/or power. God's children will also have a godly character similar to Jesus'.

The very nature of Jesus' glory is easy to miss if we think only in terms of power. A major clue to the specific meaning of Jesus' shared glory within verse 22 can be deduced from the fact that Jesus is sharing His glory with ***all*** who follow Him from all ages ***with the result that its quality enables godly unity***. Gifts of the Spirit such as power, wisdom, knowledge, miracles, healing, proclamation, prophecy, and tongues would not in and of themselves help us form a perfect godly union and are not shared equally with all Christ's followers.[192]

The glory that Jesus is sharing with *all* of His student followers (disciples) *will enable* them in the future to live in perfect loving righteous (holy) unity with God and one another just as Jesus already lives in perfect godly unity with His Heavenly Father. Therefore, when Jesus said, "I have given them the glory that you have given me ***in order that they may be "one" as we are "one"*** [John 17:22]," we come to realize that in addition to sharing His moral nature, ***He gave up His exclusive position as the Father's only son.*** Jesus is sharing His ***sonship and His Father's nature of grace and truth*** with those who follow Him. We recognize that the very essence of Jesus' glory, which He shares with all Believers, is derived from His Father's nature and His position as an only son.

Imagine how that would have sounded to the people of the first century as they considered how much more important it would be to be the only son of the Most High God in comparison even to being the only son of their greatest leader, the Roman Emperor, which would be extremely important. If you lived in the first-century Mediterranean world and the Emperor had only one son, you would have had great respect for him considering both his present and future political positions.

It brought great joy to all who were listening to God in the first century when they heard that Jesus Christ, the only son of the Most High God, had given up His exclusive right of sonship and

---

[192] Acts 1:8; 1 Cor 12-13.

was sharing it with all who learned to trust and obey His Heavenly Father out of a growing love for Them. ***Jesus had made a way for all of the Father's obedient children to have perfect godly unity with Them and one another and be loved by the Father just as Jesus is loved! What a wonderful part of the Gospel Message!***

Let's start implementing that godly unity now as we live out our physical lives helping people know God more fully and knowing that our godly unity will be perfected when we enter into God's presence. Our effort to live out godly unified lives will help many come to understand how good God really is and that He did send Jesus into our world as its savior. Godly actions coupled with godly unity produce a strong witness of God's love and grace toward all.

Looking Closely at the Meaning of "One"

In the world of the Old Testament and in Jesus' day, the Hebrew word, "one," could mean a single entity, or a group of two or more people operating as a single entity.[193] During the four hundred years leading up to Jesus' ministry and during the first century of our present era, the Greek translation of the Hebrew word, "one," within the Septuagint–when referring to unity among God's people within the Old Testament–was consistently translated into a common Greek form (masculine, feminine, or neuter) of "one" depending on which form was needed for proper grammar.[194]

We have already noted that when God created Adam and then Eve, they were created in Their image according to Their likeness (image and likeness of Us). We should note further that the Father, Son, and Holy Spirit were proclaimed to be "One" in Deuteronomy 6:4. This proclaims the "oneness/close unity" of the Father, Son, and Holy Spirit.

---

[193] Hebrew word *eḥad*, "one."

[194] Greek masculine, feminine, or neuter forms of "one": *heis, mia, hen.*

After God created Adam and Eve as male and female, we see Him saying in Gen 2:24 that they will work together in a close godly unity that we call "marriage" expressed through the Hebrew language as "one" flesh.[195] The Hebrew "one" of Gen 2:24 is translated in the Greek Septuagint as "one" flesh just as it is written in New Testament Greek of Matt 19:5.[196]

We see from God's Word that when a man and woman commit to each other in godly unity (marriage), they are committing to work together as a close godly team versus agreeing to work together as two independent beings. They are agreeing to work together in a very close godly unity with genuine concern and overall love for each other.

As other scriptures are examined, we read in verses such as Judges 20:1, 8, 11, and 1 Sam 11:7 that when Israel was attacked by others, large numbers of men came out as "one" man[197] to overcome adversity and wrongdoing. This was translated in the Greek Septuagint as "one"[198] man. The men of Israel came out as a godly close-knit team working together to overcome their common enemies. There are other examples such as in Genesis 34:16 when Jacob's sons deceptively told Shechem and his father Hamor that if they and their people would become like Israel and circumcise their males they would all become "one" people allowing them to intermarry. The Septuagint translates this part as "one" race showing that "one" was used to show a desired close oneness (unity) and was translated accordingly into the same common Greek word expressing "one" or "oneness."

As the Apostle John wrote to Gentiles in the common Greek of his day, it helps us understand Jesus' prayer for godly unity among His followers. We take note that John used the same Greek wording of the Septuagint corresponding to the Hebrew idea

---

[195] Hebrew *eḥad*, "one."

[196] Hebrew: *eḥad*; Greek: *mian* both meaning "one."

[197] Hebrew: *eḥad*, "one."

[198] Greek: *heis*, "one."

of "one/oneness." This helps us to understand that Jesus prayed for us to share in the same godly unity that He always had with His Heavenly Father and would again share with Him after His Father raised Him from dead.[199]

As John shared Jesus' prayer with others in the first century, they would have understand John to be saying that Jesus' death on a cross and the sharing of His glory would result in a godly unity for His followers that would eventually match Jesus' unity with His Heavenly Father. Through Jesus' prayer recorded in John 17, we have a clear understanding of how close we will be to God and one another at the end of the Creation in the New Heaven and on the New Earth.

Through this same prayer, God's obedient children should also understand that they should experience some of this godly unity while living out their physical lives, which helps provide a great witness that **Jesus is the Sent Son of God;** this helps our lost World understand that God sent Jesus to die for ***all*** and loves His obedient children in the same way that He loves Jesus.[200] Let's all consider the Early Church as described in Acts and strive to follow Jesus closely showing some of our future perfected godly unity, which will in turn provide a better life for us now and a better witness to the world around us that God has the best way of life for all who listen to Him now and in the future.

All Are Equal: the Father Has No Favorites

> There is neither Jew nor Greek;
> there is neither slave nor freeman;
> and there is not male *and* female;
> because *all of you are "one"* [201]
> through Christ Jesus. Gal 3:28

---

[199] Acts 2:22-36.

[200] John 17:23.

[201] The same Greek wording for unity as in John 17: *heis*, "one."

Jesus prayed that ***the children of God's eternal family would all be united in close godly unity***: they would be "one" (John 17:20-23). Paul used the same Greek root in Gal 3:28 as shown above. ***God does not have favorites*** (James 2:1-5). God has created each individual uniquely different emotionally and physically including such attributes as eye, hair, and skin color. ***Although He has created everyone with unique attributes, He wants all to work together in close godly unity*** (1 Cor 12). God's unbiased love encourages Jesus' followers to love all people equally (John 3:16; 2 Peter 3:9; 1 Tim 2:4; cf. 1 Cor 13).

The moment that we fully receive Jesus Christ into our lives as our ***lord and savior***—which means turning our lives over to the potter, who is our Heavenly Father, so that He can finish the good work that He started in us—we begin to realize our father-only-son relationship. Once we are born from above, it is a done deal. Even in our present state of sin, we become our Father's justified children who are learning to be more and more like Jesus, who eventually will be completed in His likeness. God tells us that when we have been born of the Spirit, He places His Seed, which is the Holy Spirit into us (Eph 1:13-14). When we submit to God and His way, He begets us spiritually into His eternal family, and we can no longer **continually . . . continually . . . continually** sin.[202]

As soon as we are born a second time, this time with the Holy Spirit uniting with us forever within the Family of God, our walk with God starts improving and will continue to improve over time. This helps the World see God's goodness and His great rewarding way of life more fully.

The loving righteous nature and close godly unity between the Father and the Son makes it possible to know Both by simply knowing Jesus: when you know Jesus, you also know the Father through Jesus' nature.[203] Where Jesus' followers are, Jesus and the Father are. Jesus introduces us to a third individual who is united perfectly to the Father and Him, the Spirit of Truth. If you know

---

[202] 1 John 3:9.

[203] John 14:7-11; Heb 1:3.

Jesus, you know the Father. If the Spirit of Truth lives in you, the Father and Jesus live in you through the Holy Spirit.[204]

The world continues to hear the Gospel from the Father and the Son through Jesus' obedient followers who are assisted by the Spirit of Truth, who is dwelling in them. The Father and the Son ***working together in perfect unity*** have sent the Spirit of Truth, the Holy Spirit, to comfort and guide all of Jesus' followers. This is similar to the way that the Father had sent the Holy Spirit to help Jesus during His earthly ministry (Matt 3:16-17; 4:1; John 8:29; 9:3; 16:32; cf. Isa 11:2; 61:1). When Jesus asked the Father to give His disciples a comforter to replace His physical presence,[205] ***He was making this special Father-only-Son relationship start immediately for all of His disciples through the indwelling and empowering of the Holy Spirit*** (Acts 1:8; Eph 1:13-14; cf. John 16:7).

Early Church Understanding

How did the Early Church understand the idea of Emmanuel, "God with us," and the godly unity that God desires for His children? Satan has been at work from the beginning of the Creation to keep as many people as possible from drawing close to God. But, he works even harder against those who start paying attention to God's invitation to join His eternal close loving righteous family. In his studies, Constantine Scouteris discovered that the Early Church Fathers had a sound understanding of God's desired closeness through the apostles teachings on Christ.[206]

Regarding Jesus' prayer for unity among Believers, Scouteris stated that the New Testament presents Jesus' followers

---

[204] John 14:23; Matt 25:40; Acts 9:4.

[205] John 14:16-17; 16:13.

[206] Constantine Scouteris, "The People of God-Its Unity and Its Glory: A Discussion of John 17:17-24 in the Light of Patristic Thought," *The Greek Orthodox Theological Review* 30, no. 4 (Winter 1985): 399-414.

with the possibility of realizing that ***Christ's communion (fellowship/unity) removes in the most radical way any worldly communion***. Christ's communion is the creation of a new relationship, a relationship involving God and Jesus' disciples. He went on to say that John 17 has two major themes: (1) the godly unity desired by Jesus for His followers is not only for His immediate disciples ***but also for all future disciples*** who will learn to trust Jesus through apostolic teaching and proclamation; and (2) all disciples participate in Jesus' divine glory. Scouteris wrote that these two points became a solid foundation for understanding God and His desired unity (p. 401).

From Ignatius' letter to the Philadelphians written around A.D. 107, Scouteris concluded that a radical change had occurred for God's children after Jesus' ascension: their focus had moved from a subject-object relationship to one of ***participation*** with God (p. 403). God had made a way through Jesus' atoning death for a closer relationship. In Origen's (A.D. 185-254) work titled *De Principiis*, one sees Origen teaching both the future perfection into a divine likeness and unity that Jesus had prayed for (3.6.1) and a present practical unity that expresses itself in Jesus' followers being like-minded in godly unity (1.6.2).

In light of our early Greek Fathers, Scouteris sees God the Father as an accessible divine person who generates the Son and causes the Holy Spirit to go forth establishing a unique unity within the Father's kingdom. The Father has given of His divine essence to the Son and Holy Spirit, and in return they respond in freedom and love with absolute obedience to the Father's will (p. 405-06). He noted that the Early Church Fathers could now promote unity of God's people through the unifying force of Jesus Christ. In the person of Jesus, all divisions among God's children were abolished (p. 407).

Scouteris went on to discuss Gregory of Nyssa's (A.D. 330-95) teachings regarding the divided nature of each individual due to sin derived from self-centeredness. This divided nature due to sin deprived mankind of any possibility of living in godly fellowship with God or others. But, Jesus' self-sacrifice has the potential of reestablishing God's original desired harmony bringing those who listen back into a perfect unity with Him and others (p.

411). By becoming a real man with a concrete human nature, Jesus, who was of the same nature as our Heavenly Father, took on the nature of humanity and transferred godly unity to the human level enabling the unity that Jesus prayed for all of His followers (p. 414).

Having studied the terminology of being "in" the Father and being "in" Christ from a first-century Mediterranean perspective, C. H. Dodd came to the conclusion that individuals living in the first-century Mediterranean world would have understood this type of wording to denote a unity that transcends human unity, a close godly unity.[207] He said that Jesus' prayer shows a completed picture of unity for the Father, Son, and the Son's followers with love being the key. ***It is love*** that leads Jesus' disciples to obey His commands just as He obeys His Heavenly Father's commands out of love for Him.[208] The idea of "God in us" represents the most intimate union conceivable between God and man.[209]

God's Grace & Creation Are Hard To Believe

The Gospel, "Good News" message brings *such good news* that many are afraid that it cannot possibly be true. But, it is true, and it is ***never too late*** to receive Jesus Christ into one's life as one' personal lord and savior. When one makes a conscious heart-felt acknowledgment of repentance of his or her sins and receives Jesus into his or her heart as lord as well as savior, it is known by the Father, who ***immediately reconciles*** that person to Himself as one of His sons with the same inheritance as Jesus. Eventually, when all sin is removed, the children of God will experience a close godly unity that initially was only experienced by the Father,

---

[207] C. H. Dodd, *The Interpretation of the Fourth Gospel* (New York: Cambridge University Press, 1953, reprint 1958), 187-200; cf. John 14:20.

[208] p. 196.

[209] p. 197.

Son, and Holy Spirit.[210] The Father receives ***all*** who follow Jesus as His eternal holy children ***with all the rights of Jesus, His son***, not as His servants (Gal 4:7). In fact, Jesus not only calls His followers "brothers" but also "friends [John 15:12-15]." Being loved as a family member and as a friend produces the highest level of godly love and unity possible.

Are you getting a little nervous because God is calling as many as will receive Him on His terms into His close intimate holy family? Being part of God's intimate eternal loving righteous family places one into a mutually close relationship with the Father. It sounded like heresy to Israel's religious leaders in the first-century when Jesus told them that He was God's son, because by proclaiming to be His Heavenly Father's son, He was proclaiming to be a member of God's immediate family. He had made Himself equal in family membership to the Father (John 5:18).

Does it look like the deeper we dig, the more we have taken away from God's glory by our up-and-coming mature close interactive relationship with Him? The answer is an emphatic "***no***." In reality, the deeper we look, the more we realize how loving and gracious our Heavenly Father is in working with us through His Creation even in our sinful and sometimes hostile states. Knowing that we are far from perfect makes it difficult to accept that God's Creation is headed toward a pure sinless loving interactive relationship with Him. But, this is where God's Creation is heading for all who want to be part of His holy family and receive Him as their leader striving to live out their lives according to His loving righteous way of life.[211]

God's planned perfect mutually-interactive relationship within His eternal family leaves ***nothing to separate us from Him*** in the future when all sin is removed. All of the walls/barriers that sin produces will have been torn down allowing for perfect godly unity among all members of God's eternal holy family.

---

[210] John 17:20-23.

[211] Rom 5:1-5; 1 John 2:28.

Let's faithfully follow Jesus knowing that God will finish His fantastically good Creation keeping our eyes on Jesus, who is our great eldest brother. With the Father's help and looking to Jesus for leadership, Jesus' followers can have great confidence that in the not-to-distant future, they too will have a very close godly unity with God and one another based on godly unbiased love, which produces godly righteousness, grace, and truth within the members of God's eternal holy family. While we journey with God through this part of eternity, let's all strive to show more of God's unity within our local churches and around the world. This will produce a more fulfilling life now along with a greater witness to the world as we declare the goodness of God through our godly actions as well as His words.

Chapter 6
God's Great Commission

> **Jesus spoke and said, "All authority in Heaven and on Earth has been given to me. Therefore, while sojourning (traveling through this life with God) make disciples of every nation, baptizing them in the name of the Father, the Son, and the Holy Spirit, teaching them to keep all that I commanded you. And behold! I am with you (pl) every day until the completion of the Age."**
>
> **Matthew 28:18-20**

Until this age of grace is completed, Jesus commands us to make disciples as we live out our daily lives. We are to proclaim the Gospel Message that has the power to make all people whole and help develop those who receive God into their lives as lord as well as savior. The Father, Son, and Holy Spirit are drawing all who receive Them into Their eternal holy family with its perfect godly unity.

As we continue living out our lives in God's Word, we are set freer and freer from the bondage of sin, which we impose upon ourselves through our self-centeredness and selfishness. We have all been ensnared in the past by a multitude of sins such as desire for control, temporary pleasures, material security, or something else, which stopped us from doing God's good works. But through God's grace, Jesus helps us identify and turn from our sins so that we may do our Father's will. Through Jesus Christ, we can journey along a new path, a path that leads us Home to be with God for eternity. A path that includes encouraging others to join us along the way.

We have come to understand that our permanent place of residence is not on Earth; it is in Heaven. Trusting the Creator, we expect Him to guide us Home fully conformed into Jesus' holy nature.[212] We live out this short part of eternity focused on Jesus and His leadership versus the many distractions of this world. We live with godly love growing in our hearts, which in turn radically alters our outlook toward others.

As Jesus' followers step out in faith ***growing daily in their love for God and others,*** they become more and more willing to suffer and sacrifice to help those whom God puts on their hearts. In doing so, they experience a growing inner peace and joy. ***This presents a paradox to many who are not following Jesus because without a genuine love for God and others, one would normally not experience joy by helping those who normally will not pay them back for their efforts.*** Through Jesus' followers' individual and collective good works for all, the world has a better opportunity to understand the loving caring nature of God towards everyone.

Jesus expects His followers to help others with their needs as He leads, but more importantly, He expects His followers to help others become disciples ***and*** grow in their interrelationship with God and others. ***It is Jesus' followers' honor, privilege, and duty to engage people wherever they are in their spiritual journey and help them to know well the one true God.***

As God develops a proper world-view in Jesus' followers, they realize that doing His work starts at home. Literally, joining God in His world-wide ministry starts by helping our individual families, then our local church families, then our communities, and finally the entire world. Our families, churches, and local communities are our ***daily*** mission field.

The Great Commission Is a Call To Bear Much Fruit

> **Jesus, "In this way my Father is glorified: that you bear much fruit indeed being my disciples."**
> **John 15:8**

---

[212] Trust: Eph 1:13-14; Heb 11; cf. John 3:14-17; Transformation: Phil 1:6; Rom 12:2; 8:28-30; 1 John 3:1-3.

As Jesus' followers help others to know how good God is, some who have been either directly fighting against God or who have ignored Him come to realize that the Father, Son, and Holy Spirit are caring, righteous beings, who are full of grace and truth with abundant loving-kindness toward all. ***They are truly glorious and worthy to follow!***

As Jesus' followers proclaim God's loving nature to a world that is engulfed in many deceptions and corrupted by sin, some turn from Satan and his deceptions to God for a much better life now and forever. They come to realize that spiritual warfare is ongoing (Eph 6:10-12) and learn to do their assigned parts (Eph 2:10 & more) as they join Jesus, who constantly opposes Satan and leads all who will listen against him.

Just as Jesus called many from the first century into obedient discipleship, He continues to call obedient disciples from every successive generation to proclaim the good news of His growing eternal holy family and kingdom. As Jesus' followers work together, they should be confident in God's ability and celebrate the fact that they are able to do the greatest works of the Creation because of Jesus' ongoing leadership and His finished reconciling work.[213] Jesus' followers know that the Gospel message is empowered by God through the Holy Spirit and is working in everyone's life including their own. They also know that God's way of life is the only way whereby people can find inner peace and godly joy now and forever.

The Father's main mission is also His family's main mission. The Father's main mission for His Creation is to bring as many as will obediently listen to Him into His eternal close-knit loving righteous (holy) family. With the great level of freedom that the Father has given everyone, He desires that all come to a place of turning from their individual desires and aspirations to Him and His way of life.[214] Jesus' followers do their part in helping those

---

[213] John 14:12; cf. John 7:37-39.

[214] Matt 11:28-30; Luke 9:23; 2 Peter 3:9.

who are not listening to God start listening by openly displaying God's goodness through their actions as well as their words. If those who normally are not listening start to realize how good God is, they have a better chance of paying attention to the teaching and leading of Jesus through the Holy Spirit as well as listening to Jesus' followers.

If you have not been actively helping others know how good God is and the importance of Jesus' reconciling death on a cross, ***let God show you the spiritual importance of your participation in helping to build His eternal caring family and kingdom.*** God shows all who listen the importance of putting aside personal ambitions (dying to self) and receiving the mind of Christ, which allows one to experience Jesus' joy as they help others turn to God.

Paul uses the idea of "having been crucified with Christ" to help express the idea of giving up one's personal ambitions and desires in order to help the world know God. Paul's dying to self and suffering on behalf of those who would listen to God brought him great joy (Col 1:24). This is the same for all who follow Jesus.

Jesus' life was made complete by pleasing His Heavenly Father through obediently fulfilling His assigned good works (John 4:34; Heb 2:10). He experienced great levels of inner peace and joy through consistently and obediently remaining in His Father's love. Jesus' followers may also experience this great inner peace and joy by obediently following Jesus due to His great love (John 15:10).

As we each consider how God might use us to impact others for Him, it is good to keep in mind that each one of us has a limited amount of time during our physical lives in order to help others know God, which is the most important work that anyone can do. Whether we are a farmer, business man, custodian, or something else, let's help others know how good God is as we all work together to bring as many as possible into His and our eternal loving righteous family. This is the best way that we can give back to God for all of the good that He constantly does for all people.

As we help others know God better, let's keep in mind that as Jesus' early followers proclaimed God's love, in reality, they were proclaiming His holiness, which is His loving righteous way of life. Love and righteousness go hand-in-hand. God's love establishes His standards of righteousness. Therefore, in order to proclaim the Gospel–like Jesus' first-century followers– ***Jesus' present day followers must declare God's holiness as part of the Gospel Message.***

The Gospel message declares that sin must be forsaken and eventually eradicated. The whole purpose of Jesus' atoning death is to provide purification, which results in justification, for those learning to return God's love so that they are able to live with Him within His eternal holy family. Living in loving righteousness (holiness) without sin is what makes eternal peace possible in the New Heaven (Consider Rom 8:18-23).

The Great Commission Is a Work of Love

If we do not feel some of the pain of those in need, we are not walking with God. Through God, we can start to understand and relate to the pain of others,[215] and through this empathy, ***God calls us into action***. We are called to minister to our hurting brothers and sisters both lost and saved (Luke 10:29-37).

Jesus tells us that if we take care of those in need, it is the same as taking care of Him (Matt 25:40, 45). As we help our fellow brothers and sisters who are in need, we are blessing them and our eldest brother, Jesus, the true Messiah. As we receive and work with those in need including those who are esteemed least by many, we are also receiving and working with Jesus (Matt 25:40; Luke 9:46-48). **Think about it!** If we help those in need, we are also helping Jesus.

As we implement God's great commission of love and allow Jesus to lead us, He will teach us to love as He loves ***making disciples*** of all people who will listen, baptizing them in the name of the Father, the Son, and the Holy Spirit, and teaching them ***all*** things that Jesus has taught us (Matt 28:18-20). ***There is no greater work of love!***

---

[215] Isaiah 63:9; Matt 5:3-12; 1 Cor 12:26.

Do you know people who are hurting others? ***Take them to Jesus;*** He can teach them to care. Do you know people who have just given up on life? ***Take them to Jesus;*** He can restore and strengthen them. Do you know people who look out only for themselves and their families? ***Take them to Jesus;*** He can teach them to love others as He loves. Do you have any personal needs that need special attention? ***Take them to Jesus;*** He loves you and will help.

There is ***nothing*** more important than proclaiming the truth about God's goodness. God wants us to acknowledge and experience His love by working ***together*** to unite all who listen through Jesus Christ. But beware, through the barrage and necessity of taking care of the world's physical needs, we can easily lose sight of our most important ministry, which is helping others know how much God loves them and that His way of life produces the best outcome for everyone now and in the future.

Walking with Others in the Church

> **If we are walking (living) in the Light as He (God) is in the Light, we have close fellowship with one another and the blood of Jesus, His Son, cleanses us from every sin. 1 John 1:7**

This scriptural passage clearly teaches us that ***if we do not have close fellowship with other Believers, we are not walking with God.*** In reality, we should feel close to all Believers. God helps us through the Holy Spirit learn to love each other to the point that our love overrides our fear of each other and the unknown.[216] Satan loves to use self-interests and fear to isolate us from each other. As members of God's family, we must learn to love each other as family and friends. Denominational, racial, generational, socio-economical, and political walls have all been

---

[216] 1 John 4:18: cf. 1:7; 4:10-11, 18-20; John 13:34-35; 15:12-17.

constructed through Satan's prompting as humanity has struggled against God's will. Therefore, we must come to know in our hearts that there are other Believers outside our own local church families who have accepted Jesus Christ as their lord and savior just as we have. We must allow Jesus to teach us more fully how to experience more of our "oneness," which is only possible through Him.[217] Let God help us break down the barriers that our societies perpetuate through Satan's prompting. There should be no divisions within the Body of Christ, which is the Universal Church.

Through Jesus Christ, the Father supplies the authority, resources, talent, and proper frame of mind to Jesus' followers enabling them to work together helping all.[218] It is the Holy Spirit, who works in each Believer making some of God's unity possible during our physical lives. ***May God help us*!** Through Jesus, we can learn to work together and be a great **witness** to all through our actions and words. As we faithfully follow Jesus, our fellowship with God and one another will become closer and closer.

Knowing and Employing Your Talents

> **It is God who is working in you (pl.) to desire and to work according to His good purpose. Phil 2:13**

> **We are His doing, having been created in Christ Jesus for good works, which God has prepared ahead of time in order that we may live out our lives accordingly. Eph 2:10**[219]

If a person willingly follows Jesus, our heavenly Father will give that individual a desire and the ability to do His

---

[217] John 17:20-23; Rom 12:5; 1 Cor 1:10-13; Eph 2:11-16.

[218] John 17:18, 21, 23; Acts 1:8; Eph 1:19; 3:14-20; Phil 4:13; 2 Tim 1:7; Rev 3:21.

[219] cf. James 2:14-26.

predetermined assignments. Each person in God's holy family has assignments to help our local church families and our universal Church family function more smoothly. God has gifted each person with special skills. When Jesus' followers utilize their diversity following the leading and empowerment of God, their combined output is much greater than the sum of all the individual works. This is true on local community church levels and on our combined international level through the Universal Church.

Each of Christ's disciples should be ***seeking God's perfect will*** for their lives so that they may grow into effective, loving co-members of their respective local churches. Each should seek God's will to find his or her place within their local assemblies so that their local churches may be working at peak performance in their local, regional, national, and world-wide ministries. As each of Jesus' followers pick up their individual crosses following His lead, they will learn how to utilize best their individual talents helping one another and witnessing with godly effective power to the world. Each true follower of Jesus is a new creation (2 Cor 5:17) undergoing constant training in righteousness by our Heavenly Father through the Holy Spirit and other members of his or her local church and/or universal Church (sanctification).[220]

So what about your gifts/talents from God. Many of you have already figured out what you are good at and what you are not. Nevertheless, if you are still struggling with understanding your God-given talents, there are many fairly straight forward spiritual tests available that show individuals their overall strengths and weaknesses. But, keep in mind that you should not let any test become your automatic guide to service within your local church and beyond. ***Pray and ask God to reveal His desire for your work, and He will initiate a desire in your heart to do what He has assigned you to accomplish.*** It may not match your greatest apparent skills. In reality, skills are important, but without Jesus' help no one can do any spiritual work effectively.[221] The spiritual

---

[220] John 15:1-2; Rom 6:22; Gal 5:22-23; note 2 Tim 3:16-17.

[221] Eph 6:10.

battles around us are too great for humanity without God's leading and empowerment.

Paul taught the Corinthians, that although everyone was not a great evangelist, preacher, or teacher, all had an important part in Christ's Body (1 Cor 12). Some are carpenters, others cooks, others accountants, and the list goes on. But the one task that all of Jesus' followers have is the privilege, honor, and duty of sharing the Good News about God and His ongoing creation of an eternal close-knit holy family. All of His family living on earth has the joy, honor, and responsibility of helping others know God and His Creation (witnessing).

Empowerment as Needed

In his book, *The Journey*, Billy Graham reminds everyone that when one submits to God's lordship they are not alone. ***When someone submits to Jesus Christ as lord and savior, God gives them a whole new destiny with a new purpose and power.*** Jesus' followers are given a ***new life***. This new life includes a ***new relationship*** with Him and others as a member of His eternal holy family and citizenship in the Kingdom of Heaven.[222]

If we are following Jesus, God will empower us to carry out our assigned ministries. In reality, spiritual battles are beyond our capability without Jesus leading the way and empowering us. Through Jesus Christ and the indwelling of the Holy Spirit, the Father supplies the appropriate authority, power, resources, talent, and frame of mind to each and every one of Jesus' followers. ***It is the Father and Son's empowerment working through the Holy Spirit that enables Jesus' disciples to work together effectively and joyfully ministering to a lost world.***[223]

---

[222] Billy Graham, *The Journey*, 62.

[223] Acts 1:8; Rom 8:14; Eph 3:16, 20; Phil 4:13; 2 Tim 1:7; cf. Eph 6:10-18.

Being the Light of the World

Jesus' mission is also His followers' mission. Jesus is the Light of the World: He teaches reality. After Jesus' ascension, His disciples, ***the Universal Church, became the light of the world.*** They do not minister alone. Jesus and the Father dwell in them through the Holy Spirit providing guidance and empowerment as needed.[224] If individuals reject Jesus' followers, they are in reality rejecting the Father and Son (Luke 10:16). Jesus promised not to leave His followers alone, and therefore, sent the Holy Spirit, the Helper, to guide them in all truth speaking to them the words of the Father (John 16:7, 13).

Jesus' earthly life gives everyone a perfect presentation of His Heavenly Father's nature (Heb 1:3; Col 2:9). Jesus' earthly life presented a visible ***image*** (nature) of the invisible Father (Col 1:15). If you had seen Jesus ministering during His earthly life, you had seen the very nature of His Heavenly Father at work (John 14:9). Jesus' followers are to represent God to the world (2 Cor 5:17-21).

Prior to disobeying God and being corrupted by sin, Adam and Eve were created in the image of the Father, Son, and Holy Spirit (Gen 1:26). Jesus' followers are being renewed into God's ***image*** (Col 3:10). When Jesus' followers act like Jesus, the World sees the nature of God through them. The Church led by Jesus through the Holy Spirit is the Father's only physical representation on earth (Col 2:9-10; 2 Cor 5:17-21). Jesus' followers should represent God well ***being bright godly light***, which reveals reality clearly.

As the Early Church was empowered by God and filled with the Holy Spirit, they were more willing ***to share*** with others (Acts 2:44-47). They lived out their lives in a close godly unity with one heart and mind learning to love as God loves (Acts 2:42f; 4:32f). A proper relationship with God, which is founded on a growing love for God and one another, taught them to be genuinely concerned for people who were not part of their immediate biological families. Jesus gave everything including His life to help

---

[224] John 14:23; Acts 1:8; 1 Cor 2:12-13.

everyone. Jesus is still helping all people. Out of a growing love for God and others, Jesus' followers are learning to give as the Father and Son give.

Intentional Witnessing

Through Jesus' leading of the Church through the Holy Spirit, God continually works in His Creation teaching the truth of His great love for all and the importance of following His holy way of life. God has a spiritual connection with all people starting at conception and helps them to know reality throughout life but still allows the great deceiver to tempt everyone to live life the way that they want ignoring their Creator. Many people are satisfied with a life where God is not their leader failing to realize that along with following God's leadership comes a better life that is filled with a growing love, joy, and inner peace. They fail to realize that what God wants for each is based on what is best for each instead of Satan with his deceptions, which leads to a lesser quality life and ends with eternal separation from God and His eternal holy family.

Even while under great duress and persecution at times, Jesus' first-century followers helped as many as would listen see past Satan's deceptions in order that they might see and acknowledge the realty of our loving Creator.[225] ***Every generation including our own must do the same even if the personal cost is high!*** We must come to understand within our hearts as well as our minds that ***eternal separation from God is the worst thing that can happen to anyone***. As we come to understand the importance of Jesus' command ***to make disciples***, it becomes apparent that we should understand some of the basics of sharing the truth of God's Creation with others.

Effective witnessing starts with a genuine concern about others with intentional ongoing alertness ***to share Life*** with anyone God puts before us as we go about our everyday lives. Jesus

---

[225] Examples: Col 1:24; cf. 2 Cor 4:7-11; 16-18; 1 Peter 1:6-9; Heb 10:32-39; and others.

teaches us that as we learn to trust and obey Him out of love (not fear), we will do even greater works than He did while ministering on earth because He is now with the Father leading us (John 14:12). It is our privilege and honor to introduce God to others praying that they will see His goodness and receive Him into their lives. So let's continue in the footsteps of Jesus' first-century followers continuing to work hard to make God known and rejoicing with God as some of the lost start following Jesus (Luke 15:7, 10).

Presently, Jesus' followers should be intentionally engaging their cultures in order to introduce the goodness of God and His phenomenally great plan of the Creation to all who will listen. The New Testament is full of historical occurrences where Jesus' followers helped many realize that their lives were not being lived out optimally unless they were listening to God. They helped them know God, His holy ways, and His plan for an eternal perfected loving family. Over the centuries, many others have followed Jesus and have also proclaimed the Father's righteousness and good plans for all who would listen. ***Just as the generations before us, our generation must do the same!***

The Father works with His Son, the Holy Spirit, and Jesus' followers of every generation to help everyone know the reality of His Creation including His redeeming work available to all: (1) through ***the Holy Spirit's personal teaching*** about life and the Creation;[226] (2) through ***the Holy Spirit's convicting teaching*** regarding sin, righteousness, and the judgment to come (John 16:7-11); and 3) through ***Jesus and His followers' teaching*** about God, His loving righteous way of life, and His helpful written Word, which provides opportunities for everyone to know God better.

Jesus' followers of all generations are commanded to make disciples of all people as they live out their lives (Matt 28:10-20). As they share the Gospel (the Good News) with those not following Jesus and teach about: (1) God's love; (2) abundant free will; (3) personal sin; (4) God's redeeming work; and (5) personal repentance, each one hearing the Gospel (Good News) message is personally responsible for their response.

---

[226] Rom 1:18-32; 2:11-16; cf. 1 John 2:27.

As Jesus' followers share the Good News about what God is doing through His Creation, some will experience moments of spiritual awakening. During these moments, individuals have an opportunity to realize the damaging effect of personal sin and make a conscious decision to turn from their self-centered and selfish ways to God and His loving righteous ways (repentance). Even if some do not want to listen to the Father during their spiritual awakening moments, they are required to consider Him and His way of life including the cost of submitting to Him and following Jesus. Eventually, everyone must personally decide to either receive or reject Jesus; when one chooses not to receive Him as lord and savior, that is the same as rejecting Him and our Heavenly Father.

Witnessing through Actions as Well as Words

For those whom we encounter through everyday life, our actions coupled with our words are important parts of our overall witness for God. Combined effectively, they show people how God's children love both God and them. When someone is able to demonstrate God's love through their ***actions as well as their words***, the person being witnessed to sees a fuller picture of God's love than by words alone. Therefore, it is important to witness with both actions and words whenever possible.[227]

Over the years, I have witnessed in many different circumstances including everyday interactions, various forms of ongoing ministry, and while traveling. In some cases when you do not have time to build much of a relationship, it is critically importance to show kindness and genuine concern for the other's well being. Through the Holy Spirit, this may be enough to set the stage for successful witnessing where someone listens carefully to what God is saying through you.

While living out your everyday life, you will have opportunities to demonstrate your love and concern for individuals

---

[227] Matt 5:14-16; cf. Eph 2:10; 1 John 3:18.

and/or groups, and some will want to hear what you have to say about God. They may come to understand that God cares about them and that you represent Him. In all cases, if you are able to get individuals to give you the opportunity to discuss God and His goodness, you are moving in the right direction.

Most of us have heard the phrase that "actions speak louder than words." This is an important concept for Jesus' followers to remember as they help others get to know God better. I have a friend in ministry in an area of the world where Hindus have controlled much of the population for centuries. Over the years, missionaries had come into his area and had been largely unsuccessful in getting others to follow Jesus. They shared the Good News of the One True Creator God in their polytheistic world. They proclaimed a better life now and a perfect life filled with love, joy, and peace in the future if people would turn away from their many gods and start following the Son of God, Jesus, the Messiah (Christ).

After many years of the Church not making any significant progress in this area, one of my friends and his associates were successfully able to help many know God well enough to commit to following Jesus. It was largely due to the fact that he and his fellow ministers patiently worked with the people of this area helping them ***to experience*** God's love by helping them with everyday needs including providing clean drinking water, learning personal hygiene, improving education, and helping them find better work as they simultaneously talked to them about the goodness of the One True God versus all of Satan's deceptions that kept them in bondage.

As the people saw God's love in action, they were more receptive to hear about how the Creator loves all impartially and wanted them to have a better life now and in the future following Jesus. With God's love being manifest in very tangible ways through Jesus' followers' ***actions*** along with encouraging words from the Bible, many people in this area walked away from Satan's deceptions within Hinduism and a long standing caste system and now live a much more abundant life following Jesus. Let's help others know God using both words *and* actions whenever possible!

Conversational Witnessing

In their book, *Becoming a Contagious Christian*, Bill Hybel, Lee Strobel, and Mark Mittelberg discuss how easily Jesus' followers can intentionally witness. They state that witnessing should be motivated by love.[228] Knowing that God is relational and has created His children to be relational, when we have the opportunity, we should take the time to build godly relationships looking for opportunities to discuss God's great love and corresponding righteous actions for all. As already noted several times, it is also important to remember that most of the people whom we come in contact with notice ***what we do*** as well as ***what we say***. Therefore, it is important to live a loving righteous life that accurately expresses God's caring nature.

Later in their book, they discuss how one should look for ways within everyday conversations to move from the natural to the spiritual realm. In addition, they discuss the importance of looking for ways to build a communication bridge from the physical realm to the spiritual realm (pp. 135ff). In some cases, individuals have already started listening to the Holy Spirit and are eager to discuss God. But normally, you will need to figure out how to ***transition*** the conversation from the natural to the spiritual in order to have any real discussion about God. It is good somewhere fairly early in a witnessing conversation to come up with a statement or pose a question involving God to see if the other person has any desire to speak about spiritual matters. It could be as simple as saying something like, "I do not know what I would do without God's guidance and help." If the person is receptive, then you will be able to develop a spiritual conversation through God's leading to see how far you should continue the spiritual part of your conversation.

With so many things going on in our lives, the most important part of witnessing is being willing and intentionally open

---

[228] Bill Hybels and Mark Mittleburg, *Becoming a Contagious Christian* (Grand Rapids: Zondervan, 1994), 67ff; cf. John 3:16-17; 2 Cor 5:14; 1 John 4:10-19.

to God's leading at all times throughout each day. ***Be intentionally ready to initiate a spiritual conversation!*** Then as the Holy Spirit leads, be sensitive to the length and depth of each witnessing encounter. I have had times where I have felt God's leading to speak to someone about Him for only a few minutes, and at other times, I have spoken for hours. God will show you through the other's actions and words how long and on what level you should discuss Him. From my personal experiences, it has normally been fairly straightforward to start a spiritual discussion based on personal or shared events. In many cases, as you are developing a closer relationship with someone, God will help you make timely transitions from everyday secular conversations into spiritual discussions.

As you are developing godly relationships with others, it is also good to introduce them to others who are also followers of Jesus so that they are able to see more clearly what following Jesus might look like. For some, it may be as easy as simply inviting them over to your house to meet some Christian friends or asking them to join you at church, or come to Bible studies, and/or special Christian events such as an Easter celebration.

There are many helpful books and videos available that discuss the various ways to witness ***intentionally*** to others. A couple additional books to consider are Bill Hybels' *Just Walk Across the Room*, and Dick Innes' *I Hate Witnessing*.[229] If you ask God to help you tell others about how good He is and how His way of life brings about the best outcomes, now and forever, He will help you witness more effectively taking into consideration everyone's unique personalities and experiences.

---

[229] Bill Hybels, *Just Walk Across the Room: Simple Steps Pointing People to Faith* (Grand Rapids: Zondervan, 2006).

Dick Innes, *I Hate Witnessing: A Handbook for Effective Christian Communications*. rev. ed. (San Clemente: Acts Communications, 2003).

Important Words and Concepts

When presenting the Gospel to someone, you should be sensitive to that person's present understanding of God. The range can vary significantly from some who are deceived to the point of thinking that there is no Creator to those who know that God exists and loves them deeply, but they do not want to submit to His leadership (lordship). When we speak to others about God, we need to remember that everyone is unique. We should be prepared to customize our Gospel presentations including our personal testimony in such a way as to be most effective in reaching each person within their present spiritual state of mind. God will help us with this.

In any and all cases, there are some basic biblical principles discussed below that everyone should know. Everyone should be ready to discuss the basics of God's ample free-will Creation and His ongoing redemptive work, which is based on His impartial love and redemptive work that is available to all no matter how bad someone has been. Many of the passages supporting these foundational truths do not need to be memorized, but there are some that you should be familiar with as discussed below.

In most Gospel presentations, it is normally good to start with a brief overview of God's Creation as described in Genesis chapters one through three. The main purpose of the Creation was to create a loving righteous volunteer family for God. Mankind was created in God's image according to His likeness (Gen 1:26-27) with the ability to obey or disobey Him (Gen 2:16-17; 4:5-7 & others). God is ultimately seeking an eternal mutually reciprocating relationship with His maturing children. The first couple, Adam and Eve, chose to disobey God (Gen 3:6) separating all humanity for a short time from a close relationship with Him (Gen 3:22-24). With God knowing all things in advance prior to starting the physical part of the Creation, the Father and Son worked out a plan through Jesus' atoning death that would remove all bad actions (sin) from those who would receive Them into their lives as lord and savior (Rom 10:9-13; Acts 2:22-39; Ps 103:12; Gal 3:13-14; Col 2:13-14; 2 Cor 5:21; 1 Peter

2:24; cf. John 3:14-17; Matt 26:36-46). When God finishes adding new members to His eternal holy family, he will finalize His Creation in perfection, which includes a final combined eternal spiritual and physical state (resurrected body) for those who become part of His family (Phil 3:20-21; cf. 1 Thess 4:13-17) and eternal separation from Him for all who do not (2 Peter 3:7; Rev 20:11-15).

The heart of the Gospel message is about how Jesus, the Son of God, the long awaited Anointed One (Messiah), willingly died on a cross suffering shame, excruciating physical pain, and excruciating spiritual pain (complete separation from His Heavenly Father) after taking on the bad actions of all who turned to God throughout the entire Creation making it possible for all who learn to love, trust, and obey God to live eternal sinless lives (Rom 8:28-30; cf. Heb 1:2-3; 2 Cor 5:21; 1 Peter 2:24). This incredible miracle came at a great cost to God through the suffering and separation of the Father and Son during the Son's three days in Hades (Sheol) paying the penalty for our sins (separation from His Heavenly Father). The Good News is that although ***all*** have sinned and fallen short of living in godly perfection (Rom 3:23), everyone of all ages can be made complete with total sin removal by learning to return God's love (Rom 6:22-23; 1 John 4:10-16; cf. Rom 10:4), which includes trusting and obeying Him (John 3:16; 36; 14:23; 15:10).

With a growing love, trust, and obedience, individuals have a better chance to turn from self-centeredness to God and His way of life (repentance: 2 Peter 3:9) and ask God to forgive their sins and lead their lives (1 John 1:9 & more). Once they receive God into their lives as lord and savior, they are brought into His eternal intimate holy family through spiritual birth (John 1:11-13; 3:3, 5; Eph 1:13-14). They become new creations (2 Cor 5:17) gaining the mind of Christ (1 Cor 2:16). Having the mind of Christ and being part of God's eternal close-knit holy family, Jesus' followers joyfully do their part (John 17:13 & more) in leading others to God so that as many as possible will receive God into their lives as lord as well as savior and thereby become part of His eternal holy family (saved) (Matt 28:18-20). Eventually all who learn to return God's love and willingly follow His leadership will be in His eternal presence in the New Heaven and on the New Earth (Eph 1:13-14; Rom 10:9).

In addition to the Scripture references noted above, ***here are some important Scripture references shown below that everyone should be familiar with.*** Some of the most important Scripture references have asterisks placed in front of them. If you do not have these critical verses memorized, prayerfully consider doing so.

- **God Is Creating a Close-Knit Eternal Holy Family, which is the Crown Jewel of His Creation (John 3:3, 5; 17:11, 20-23; Rev 21:1-6)!**

- **With abundant free will came disobedience with its bad actions (sin); God's main message to all has been to turn from sin to His way of a caring righteous life, which is called repentance (Matt 3:2; 4:17; Acts 2:38; *2 Peter 3:9)!**

- **Jesus' followers proclaim that Jesus is the only way to eternal life *with* God through repentance (*John 14:6)!**

- **Jesus' atoning death on a cross provides the Way for all who learn to trust and obey God out of a growing love for Him to be with Him & one another forever without sin (*John 3:14-17, 36; 14:21, 23; *2 Cor 5:21; 1 Peter 2:24; cf. Gal 3:13-14; Col 2:13-14) and is available for all who receive Him and His way of life (John 1:11-13; *Rev 3:20)!**

- **Jesus' followers grow in their love, trust, and obedience as they step out in faith doing the good works that have been assigned to them prior to the physical creation of the world (*Eph 2:10; Matt 28:18-20; Heb 5:14).**

If you run across individuals who are not sure about their salvation, ask them if they remember a time when they asked God for forgiveness of their sins and told Him that they would gladly follow Jesus wherever He leads. If the answer is "no," then they need to do so as soon as they are ready. If the answer is "yes," then they should already be new creations and part of God's eternal close-knit holy family.[230] With this being the case, ask if they have noticed a change in their lives since starting to follow Jesus that includes things like wanting to please God; living more loving and righteous lives over time as our Heavenly Father develops them; experiencing a growing concern for others; being happy when someone starts to follow Jesus; and not being afraid of the coming judgment. No one has or will live a perfectly sinless physical life other than Jesus, but everyone who is following Jesus should want to please God and their overall lives should reflect a developing loving righteous walk with God and man. If their answer is "no," then they should seek God's help through prayer and godly action to improve their relationship with Him.

Stepping Out in Faith in Our Local Communities

God asks each of Jesus' followers to help others on individual, family, local-church, and community-wide levels as part of their ***daily*** lives. Although our Heavenly Father is not asking all of Jesus' followers to go into full-time ministry, ***He is asking all to step out in faith and become involved.*** As followers of Jesus listen to Him, they do their assigned parts helping their local church families proclaim the Gospel. Through prayer, seeking utilization of godly talent, and ministering under Jesus and His appointed local overseers, our Heavenly Father helps Jesus' followers serve others individually and collectively.

Once an individual has made a genuine commitment to follow Jesus Christ, there is only one thing left to do: ***do it!*** We are justified and empowered only when we ***trust and obey*** the Sent

---

[230] Eph 1:13-14; 2 Cor 5:17.

Son. Therefore, let us ***joyfully do*** our assigned works, not out of resentment nor fear but out of a growing love for God and others. It is critical for Jesus' followers ***to step out in faith and actually follow Him. Implementation matters!***

If you do not follow through and implement your plans and investments, they will never do you any good! Failure to implement God's plans is constantly occurring in our contemporary local churches. Many are meeting on a regular basis with others and making plans to get serious about their walk with Jesus. But, through Satan's deceptions, personal desires, and many forms of busyness most do not implement their commitment by stepping out in faith and truly following Jesus.

When you are inspired by God to make a change in your life, make a commitment to follow God's lead and quickly step out in faith to live accordingly. If you fail to step out in faith when God inspires you, there is a good chance that you will forget that inspiration within a relatively short time and not do what God laid on your heart.

Being Committed

It takes courage and commitment to step out in faith and proclaim God's Word when it is unpopular, but under God's leadership and empowerment, some will listen and be saved. A German, Dietrich Bonhoeffer, was a faithful follower of Jesus during the years leading up to and during WWII and was martyred in a concentration camp located at Flossenburg on April 9, 1945 just before the end of the war in Europe.[231] Bonhoeffer's life was one of engaging his culture and speaking out against the terrible things that Hitler and many of the German leaders were doing. Many of his own countrymen would not speak out against Hitler either because of fear of loss including their lives or possible loss of personal gain that might be obtained by following him.

---

[231] Dietrich Bonhoeffer, *Letters & Papers from Prison*, rev. ed., ed. Eberhard Bethge (New York: Simon & Schuster, 1997), 411.

Bonhoeffer called many of His countryman to task for not following Christ's teachings and wrote a book titled *The Cost of Discipleship* reminding people that following Jesus required commitment and action.[232] After being imprisoned and his life became more difficult, Bonhoeffer came to realize that following Jesus depended wholeheartedly on turning one's life over to God. He came to realize that repentance was a true turning to God and that Jesus' followers need to live out life trusting God in all circumstances. ***By turning to God and depending on Him in all circumstances, one became a true follower of Jesus, a renewed man of God.*** He came to realize that God– no matter what the circumstances –would lead him and all of Jesus' followers home to Himself.[233]

Let's All Follow Jesus!

Jesus commanded it, and His early disciples did it. They worked well together proclaiming God's Grace bringing many to God. Throughout the New Testament, we take note that Jesus' disciples expressed their godly unity (oneness) through their common fellowship and ministry. Initially, Believers waited together for empowerment from God through the Holy Spirit;[234] after being empowered, they ministered together with one heart and mind providing a great witness,

> **All those who were believing in/trusting (God) were together and having all things in common, and their possessions and property they were selling and dividing these things to each one according to whatever he or she had need; and**

---

[232] Dietrich Bonhoeffer, *The Cost of Discipleship* (New York: Touchstone, 1995).

[233] Bonhoeffer, *Letters & Papers from Prison,* 369-370.

[234] Acts 1:14.

> **throughout each day they were together of one mind in the Temple, and breaking bread from house to house, receiving (eating) food with great joy and humility of heart praising God and having grace for all people. And the Lord was placing those who were being saved throughout each day together. Acts 2:44-47**

They did not sell **all** their possessions, **nor** was it mandatory to sell any of their possessions to be part of the Universal Church (Acts 5:4). In reality, first-century followers of Jesus still had personal property including homes.[235]

But, we observe that as Jesus' followers were filled with the Holy Spirit (born from above, born of the Spirit), they were more willing ***to share*** their possessions with others. A proper relationship with God, which is built on godly love, taught Jesus' followers to be genuinely concerned for people who were not part of their immediate biological family.

Jesus gives all Believers one heart and mind so that they can journey with God and one another in godly unity "oneness" [John 17:11, 20-23]. We note that the Church was ministering with great grace as Jesus' followers sold their excess and gave it to those in need. If we wish to live in God's will today, we must do likewise. We must learn to have genuine concern for everyone and help those whom God asks us to help. God will teach us to help those who are not part of our immediate biological family both spiritually (godly relationships) and physically.

Our greatest witness will be at its best when we come to realize more fully who we are in Jesus Christ and begin to act accordingly as the reconciled children of God that we are. We must come to understand deeply that separation from God ***is the worst thing*** that can happen to anyone and that those not listening to God are part of our family and need rescuing (Acts 17:26-28; 2 Peter 3:9 & more).

---

[235] Property & Control of Resources: Acts 5:4. Owning Personal Houses: Acts 12:12.

Chapter 7
Sojourning & the Universal Church

> **. . . And the land shall not ever be sold because the land belongs to me, (and) because you are temporary dwellers and sojourners with me; . . . .**
> **Leviticus 25:23[236]**

> **For our place of citizenship exists in [the] heavens out of which we are awaiting a savior, the Lord Jesus Christ . . . . Phil 3:20**

We are just traveling through. We are sojourning with God as we join him in His great work of love that He established for His Son and us from the beginning of the Creation.[237] When we receive God as lord and savior through Jesus Christ, we become fully reconciled children beginning our role as His ambassadors and priests.[238] Although we all belong to various earthly kingdoms, our eternal kingdom and citizenship is with God in Heaven.[239] As His ambassadors and priests on earth, we are to proclaim Truth (reality) and act as mediators between God and man. We are not to settle down and become satisfied using our blessings from God solely for ourselves and our families. We have come to recognize that our physical life is only a short fraction of our eternal life, and that we have been called to be co-laborers with God.

---

[236] Translated directly from the Masoretic Hebrew Text, *Biblia Hebraica Stuttgartensia* (Germany: Alle Rechte vorbehlten, 1987).

[237] Eph 2:10; 2 Tim 1:8-9; Titus 2:14.

[238] Exod 19:5-6; 2 Cor 5:17-6:1; 1 Peter 2:9-10; cf. 1 Cor 3:9.

[239] Phil 3:20-21; Rev 21:1-7.

We have been fully reconciled to God with all the emotional and legal rights of direct descendants of the Creator. We have an ***eternal perfect home*** with God awaiting us, and we know that in a short time the rewards, trials, and challenges of this age shall be over. How can it possibly be better? It is exceeding good because God has called us into His work as co-laborers. ***We are not just spectators watching a performance from the sidelines!*** We are full-time co-laborers with the Creator as He ministers to all humanity spiritually (relationally) and physically. He grows us spiritually as we learn to listen to Him and join Him in His ministry.[240] As we work with God, He grows our heart to match His as He works with us transforming us to be like Jesus.

Jesus' followers work under His and His sub-shepherds' authority ministering to all people. Their individualized work varies according to their God-given abilities and God's corresponding position for each person within His eternal holy family. Their godly unity and work involves everything from praying to physically ministering around the world. All of God's work provides great blessings to His obedient children as they work with those who are not listening to Him encouraging them to repent and come Home.

The Universal Church

As Paul proclaimed the Good News of God's interactive plan of redemption that was available to all, he also proclaimed ***that the risen Lord Jesus was the active lord of the world-wide Church.*** He told Jesus' followers at Corinth, "You are the Body of Christ, indeed *a member of a part of the whole* [1 Cor 12:27]." The followers at Corinth were all part of the local assemblies (churches) within their city, which was a part of the entire world-wide Body of Christ, the Universal Church. As the various local assemblies grew within their cities, they were reminded that they were all part of the whole, the Body of Christ.

---

[240] Matt 7:21; John 5:19 & 15:5; John 16:13 & Rom 8:14; 1 Cor 3:9.

After Jesus died on the Cross for all humanity and ascended into Heaven to rule at His Father's right hand, we see a major shift from the national religious leaders of Israel to Jesus and His followers, who collectively are the new Israel. Within the first twenty years after Jesus' ascension, many Gentiles had begun following Israel's long awaited prophesied Messiah (Christ). Within thirty years, Paul said that the Gospel had been made known to all nations (Rom 16:26), which shows that many Gentiles of various nations especially in the Mediterranean world had already heard the Good News about what our Heavenly Father had done through His Son, Jesus and a fair number had started following Jesus putting aside Satan's false gods.

And, just as Jesus had forewarned many of Israel's religious leaders during His earthly ministry, the Father removed their authority and gave it to another group of leaders and people, who now consisted of Judeans (Jews) and Gentiles (the rest of the world) who actively followed Jesus. Those ungodly religious leaders lost their authority, the Temple, and their beloved Jerusalem because they failed to listened to the very son of God, Jesus, due to their hardened hearts toward God and man.

With Jesus' victorious ascension, the Father placed Him at His right hand. He was the Eternal High Priest (Heb 7:1-8:6). When the Creation is finished, everyone saved and unsaved will submit to the lordship of Jesus, who after judging the ungodly at the great white throne judgment (John 5:22, 30; Rev 20:11-15), will then hand everything over to the Father and everyone will recognize the Father as the overall leader of all (1 Cor 11:3; 15:28; cf. John 14:28).

During Jesus' present reign over the Heavens and Earth, the Universal Church, His Body, represents Him on Earth. The Church is no longer obligated to keep the nation of Israel's ordinances that regulated Israel's cultural norms nor the sacrificial laws, which were fulfilled through Jesus' atoning death. This allows the Universal Church with its god-given holy unity to follow the eternal moral lifestyle of God within all cultures as long as those cultural practices do not violate God's moral standards (Rom 2:11-16). Wherever God's people live, they are expected to live according to His moral standards caring for all.

Denominational, racial, generational, socio-economical, and political walls have all been constructed through Satan's prompting as humanity with its abundant free will has struggled against God, His authority, and His good plans for everyone. Jesus' followers should be dismantling these walls within their local churches and their cultures as they live out their lives. It is important that Jesus' followers learn to take pleasure in allowing our Heavenly Father to teach them how to love as He loves. All of Jesus' followers worldwide should seek to live in godly unity as members of the same eternal holy family. The Universal Church is the part of God's eternal holy family that is presently living on Earth. ***It needs to act accordingly!***

Our Local Churches

The Church first and foremost is the holy Family of God! All true followers of Jesus Christ are part of the same Kingdom and have the same Sustainer living in them (Eph 4:1-6). Jesus' followers comprising the various assemblies/churches at the local community level should be striving for a high level of godly unity within their congregations, cities, and the Universal Church.

Members of local assemblies should learn to care enough for one another that they are able to be more transparent than the world when interacting with one another without being concerned about sensitive information being used against them at later times. But, due to unbelief and immaturity, many members within local churches still hurt one another on a regular basis. For those who are reasonably mature followers of Jesus, the door is open for a rich relationship with other like-minded Christians.

How can a local church be effective in taking care of its own members or reaching out to the lost if there is little peace and joy within their local church? If your local church is not experiencing at least a little godly unity with God and one another, you and your fellow members need to fast, pray, and read God's Word together seeking His help in removing sin and walking more closely with Him until He gives you a spiritual breakthrough.

Members of congregations who are walking closely with God will experience great love, joy, inner peace, and excitement as they minister to one another and the world around them bringing those who will listen into a saving relationship with God and one another.

Being Social

As godly social beings, we should be volunteering in order ***to do our part*** within the holy Family of God. When members of the family are all doing their part, things go more smoothly and everyone experiences more godly unity and joy. Consider living at home for a moment. Think of the importance of parents teaching their children to do their part.

If children do not learn to help with the basic work around the house and yard, they hinder their families and grow up with a personal handicap in managing and taking care of their own future families. It is important within families for each capable member to do his or her part. If some are not socially responsible in helping, others have to do more than they should. This ungodly action causes the entire family to suffer.

This is contrary to God's desire for our personal families, His local church families, and even His world-wide Holy Family, the Universal Church. If we are not experiencing some level of godly unity and social responsibility within our local churches, we should seek our Heavenly Father's help in learning the importance of following Jesus' leadership. ***It is only through our obedience to Jesus' leadership that we will learn to work together in a godly fashion.*** If Jesus does not hold first place within our own hearts and the hearts of our local church leaders, it does not take long for our local churches to become self-seeking and spiritually ineffective individually and collectively within our communities.

Developing & Multiplying Disciples

> **And Christ gave on the one hand apostles, but on the other prophets, evangelists, pastors, and teachers for the establishing of His Holy Ones (Saints) for the work of the Ministry for the building up of the Body of Christ, until we all come, to the unity of faith and knowledge of the Son of God, to a perfect (complete) man, to a measure of the maturity of the fulness of Christ.**
>
> **Eph 4:11-13**

As we come to the place of wanting Jesus to lead us, He helps us know and do the good works that our Heavenly Father set for each of us during the planning stages of the Creation. A great part of that work is developing God's holy family so that ***Jesus' followers can collectively take care of one another and become productive helpful witnesses to the lost world around them.*** God wants those who are more mature in His family to help train those who are less mature. After leading people to Jesus, it is very important that the more mature teach the less mature how to live out ***all*** that Jesus commanded.

In his book, *The Journey*, Billy Graham reminds us that people who have recently turned to follow Christ are in reality like newborn children regarding their understanding of spiritual things.[241] There may be barriers to spiritual growth such as continuing sin, ungodly pressure from family members, friends, or associates, or uncertainty in what is expected.[242] Jesus' more mature followers should be teaching and guiding those who are

---

[241] Billy Graham, *The Journey: How To Live by Faith in an Uncertain World* (Nashville: W Publishing, 2006), 74-76.

[242] Graham, *The Journey*, 77-78. For a practical introduction to discipleship, consider working through Henry Blackaby's 13 week course, *Experiencing God*, rev. ed. (Nashville: Broadman and Holman, 2008).

less mature (mentorship). It is a privilege for the more mature to help the less mature grow more and more into the likeness of Jesus.

It is Jesus' more mature followers' duty, honor, privilege, and joy to help those who are less mature grow in their understanding and walk with Him and others.[243] Jesus' more mature followers should provide regular times of collective worship, small group meetings, Bible studies, specialized discipleship classes, and times of active ministry to help the entire Body grow. If the mature members of our local churches do not help make and develop new disciples *including their own children*, how will future generations know God and His way of life?

God's Leadership and Our Local Communities

As we examine the organizational structure of the Universal Church in the New Testament looking for guidance for our current ministries, we note that many evangelized cities had a council of elders appointed by Jesus through the apostles. The apostles also provided initial encouragement and guidance to the various city-councils.

Initially, the local church in Jerusalem gave the final rulings on doctrinal issues that came up before the Universal Church (sum of all local churches worldwide). We note that God did not specify any specific form of worship in the New Testament for individual assemblies. In addition, we observe great cooperation among first-century Believers everywhere. Jesus' followers proclaimed God's grace through their ***actions*** and ***words*** bringing many of their time to repentance and salvation.[244] Through Jesus' leadership, they helped many in their world come to know the One True God who had created everything and loved everyone instead of following a multitude of false satanic gods.

---

[243] Matt 28:20; Acts 2:42.

[244] Matt 9:13; Acts 2:38-41; 4:4; etc.

After Jesus' ascension, He continued to guide the Church through the Holy Spirit. Each community acted as a living organism helping others. In the earliest stages of Universal Church growth, we observed the apostle Peter acting as a spokesman in Jerusalem. Later, Peter was forced to flee for his life,[245] and it appears that the apostle James was given the role of spokesman.[246] As the Church grew, we note an important trend: Jesus continually expanded the leadership of the Universal Church to accommodate its growth with the local church at Jerusalem establishing Church doctrine for all of the local churches throughout the Mediterranean world and beyond until God's Word was expanded to include a collection of inspired New Testament writings by later Universal Church councils.

As we evaluate the early Church's growth, we take special notice that Jesus remained the leader. We observe Jesus working through Paul and Barnabas appointing elders on their second pass through Lystra, Iconium, and Antioch of Syria (Acts 14:21-23). When Paul traveled to Jerusalem on his third missionary journey, he stopped in Meletus and summoned the elders of the assembly (Called-Out Individuals/Believers) of Ephesus and reminded them that the ***Holy Spirit*** had appointed them as overseers (Acts 20:17, 28). We learn through these accounts and others that elders (presbyters) of a city-church council were the same as overseers (episcopates/ bishops) and pastors. There were four basic terms used throughout the New Testament showing three levels of authority. The four terms and three levels of authority are: Lord; apostles; overseers (elders, pastors) of local assemblies and city-wide councils, and deacons. Deacons assisted as needed and did not have organizational authority. Jesus was and is the leader (lord) of all, which is His Body on earth.

---

[245] Acts 12:1-17.

[246] Gal 1:18-19; Gal 2:1-10. When Paul went up to Jerusalem 17 years after his Christian conversion, he lists three existing pillars of the Christian community, the apostles James, Peter, and John. Paul lists James first, which indicates that James was the main spokesman at that time.

Generally, the term "deacons," referred to anyone who served others. The list of deacons is fairly extensive starting with Jesus (Rom 15:8); the Apostles (Acts 6:1-2,4); and Paul.[247] Then stepping outside the Church, we observe Paul telling the local church residing in Rome that all civil rulers are also God's deacons (Rom 13:4). Even Satan has deacons (servant- ministers) (2 Cor 11:15).

On one level, all of Jesus' followers are automatically deacons. Yet, there is a special group of deacons discussed in Paul's first letter to Timothy. These deacons helped with the day-to-day administration of the local churches for each city. They were not required to preach the Gospel, teach, nor have the same level of administrative capabilities as the apostles or the elders who served on each of the city-councils. From Paul's letter to Timothy, we can assume that their office was set up primarily to serve the overseers in whatever capacity that they were willing and capable (1 Tim 3:1-13).

Throughout the New Testament, we observe Jesus appointing elders through His apostles such as Paul and then helping them develop so that they could lead their respective communities.[248] We observe two levels of organization with Jesus Christ being the active leader of the Church setting Church Doctrine initially through His followers in Jerusalem. Through Jesus Christ and the Holy Spirit's guidance, Jesus appointed the apostles who were responsible for evangelizing (e.g. Gospels- first twelve & Gal 1:1, 19- Paul's appointment & James, Jesus' brother) and establishing leaders within local assemblies/churches (e.g. Acts 14:21-23; 2 Cor 11:28; Titus 1:5), who worked together in their

---

[247] Acts 20:24; 21:19; Rom 11:13; 15:31; 2 Cor 6:3-4; & more.

[248] A good example of Paul's ministry as an overseer to the overseers is shown as he encourages the Corinthians to complete a promise they had made regarding sending some of their resources to help their needy brothers and sisters in Jerusalem (2 Cor 8-9).

respective communities through city-wide councils.[249] The councils of elders were responsible for collectively ministering to the day-to-day needs of their respective communities (e.g. Acts 20:17-38). The official capacity of deacons was to assist the leaders of the local churches as needed (e.g. Acts 6-7).

Today, Jesus Christ continues to guide us through the Holy Spirit and uses His written Word to establish Church doctrine. The same Holy Spirit who inspired the authors of Scripture helps Jesus' follower from all subsequent generations interpret correctly the Scriptures.[250] Jesus Christ set up the "council-of-elders" as the fundamental form of leadership for the collective ministry of all of His followers within their respective communities.

Jesus has not given us a new commandment to change this form of leadership, nor has He changed the importance of community-wide ministries. He wants to guide us as we minister on community-wide levels around the world. When a community does not have a council of elders working together, it suffers from a lack of strong Christian cooperation. Without Church leadership working together in our respective communities, Jesus is not exalted nor proclaimed as clearly nor effectively as God desires.[251]

We know that Jesus desires all of us to put some of our time in community-wide ministry. Knowing our ***identity*** and overall ***mission*** through Jesus helps us to accept our "good works" from the Father as Jesus leads us in our individual, family, local-church, community-wide, and worldwide ministries.[252] God's love, which is continually demonstrated through His ongoing good work assigned to each of us, compels us to learn to work together in godly unity at times and to serve each other all of the time.

---

[249] Note that several of Paul's letters were addressed to the councils of elders of specific cities or cities within an area such as Galatians.

[250] 2 Tim 3:16-17; 2 Peter 1:20-21; 1 John 2:27; Paul's letters are valued on the same level as Old Testament Scriptures: 2 Peter 3:16.

[251] John 13:34-35; 17:21, 23; 1 John 1:7.

[252] 1 Cor 3:9; Eph 1:4-6; 2:10; Titus 2:14.

When we come together to minister more effectively on community-wide levels, we will have to learn to put aside some of our denominational differences. If we do not allow Satan to tempt us into using our diversities to build walls, Jesus will use our diversities to strengthen our collective ministries to the point that we will be a greater witness as we join God in bringing His Creation to its final form.[253]

We are created with individual differences that can be united under Jesus' leadership to give the Universal Church great ministering power. Our denominational differences represent a rich tapestry of Christian struggle and development that can be united for ministry through Jesus into something good and powerful enhancing and highlighting the rich tapestry of all of God's children for all to see.

Coming from our different denominational, racial, socioeconomic, and generational backgrounds, we can bring great strength to our collective ministries as we allow Jesus to lead us. We can still maintain our different organizational histories, structures, and forms of worship as we ***boldly*** work together in godly unity within our communities proclaiming that the best life now and in the future is always through following Jesus. As we work together under Jesus' direction within our city-wide councils, our joint-efforts will proclaim God's love clearly to all people and bring God's transforming power to all who listen.

To work together as Christians across denominational lines under Jesus' leadership, we must all believe at least seven fundamental truths, or we will be standing collectively on a very shaky foundation and not do well. We must all believe that: 1-3) ***Jesus is the Son of God, who being of the same essence as our Heavenly Father created the physical world*** (John 1:1-3; Phil 2:6-8; Heb 1:2-3; Col 1:16-17), and 4) ***Jesus is the only Way to be reconciled to the Father and one another*** (John 14:6; cf. John 1:29 & more); and 5-7) ***we must trust God and be willing to obey Him believing*** that He has given us an ***inspired*** Book of Life, the ***Bible***, to establish

---

[253] No Divisions: 1 Cor 1:10-13; 12:25-26; Eph 2:13-15; 4:1-6.

truth (reality) to live by and that ***all*** of it is ***good*** to teach everyone about Him and His holy ways (Ps 119:104-106; 2 Tim 3:16).

In order to work together properly under Jesus' leadership, we must believe that our Heavenly Father has given us salvation through Jesus alone and that all of His Word is divinely inspired, and therefore, profitable for us to follow faithfully. As collective groups within our cities and around the world, we know that we will not agree on every theological point, but we must agree on the basics as shown above in order to make godly progress under Jesus' leadership.

No matter how large or small a church is, each church must be able to have an active voice in the decision making process and enter into collective ministries and activities as it feels led by God. No church should be looked-down-on because it chooses not to participate in some or even all of the collective community-wide activities. By allowing every Christian church to have an equal voice in discussing, promoting, and participating in community-wide ministries, it allows a true sense of equality among churches, and it allows the larger churches to serve the needs of smaller churches and their neighborhood ministries. Those who are more capable should be willing to serve those who are less able. Remember that the ultimate goal is to join God as He ministers to our individual and collective needs.

Throughout Scripture, we observe the importance of community-wide ministries. When we allow Jesus Christ to empower us so that we can serve our communities collectively, we have the greatest ability to meet the needs of all people.

In reality, each of our communities should function as a living organism similar to our local church families, individual families, and our personal lives. If we allow God to guide us utilizing His Written Word as our core foundation, He will teach all of us to minister on all levels including the highly effective community-wide level through city councils. Knowing that the people of our own communities are truly our closest neighbors, let's work together in godly unity, which will in turn be a blessing to all through our individual and collective ministries. This produces the greatest witness to the world around us.

Closing Thoughts

Most of us sense that life is something more than a fleeting time on earth prior to death. ***That is because life is eternal.*** God the Creator, who is eternal, created the angels and humanity as abundantly free-will eternal beings. Each has to decide whether or not they want to live with a loving God (Sustainer) *under His authority* or be isolated from Him and like-minded beings forever.

When we consider the big picture, we want to thank God for His loving kind righteous (holy) nature and for creating us to be an intimate part of His eternal holy life. The Father, Son, and Holy Spirit comprise a living "oneness," a godly unity, that is held together with perfect love absent of all sin. There are no divisions or walls within their intimate holy relationship. We were created in God's image according to His likeness to be part of Their intimate holy family experiencing the same godly unity with Them and one another. Through our God-given abundant free will, everyone has some sin in their lives and struggles against self-centeredness and selfishness, but God works with all from every generation helping those who listen to Him turn from their self-centered ways of life to His holy way of life bringing them into His eternal holy family.

God's desire for everyone is to choose good over evil (being hurtful). In one sense, life is simpler than we imagine, because each individual's decision regarding living for self or community determines his or her own eternal destiny. For those who choose to receive God as lord and savior, they are choosing good over evil. They are choosing what is good for others ***and*** for themselves. For those who choose self ***over*** others, they are choosing an emptier life that leads to an eternal life of shame, unrest, and suffering.

As each of us journey through this part of eternity, God reveals Himself in a multitude of ways over time wanting all to know Him (spiritual awakenings). To know God personally helps one to submit to Him and confidently and joyfully follow His leadership. Until one starts to know how good God is and how great a love that He has for all, it is easier to follow a self-centered path without submitting to Him. But, once an individual has started paying attention to God's revelation of reality through the Creation itself, His written Word, and the work of the Holy Spirit, many of Satan's deceptions and his or her own personal self-centered desires become clearer making it much easier to submit to God's leadership and way of life. His unbiased love for all shown through everything that He does helps those who listen realize that He is a loving holy father and sustainer, who is worthy of love, respect, and honor (reverence).

Can you think of anything more glorious than God and His eternal close-knit holy family? I cannot! What a privilege and honor to be invited into God's holy eternal family to be loved by our Heavenly Father as much as He loves Jesus. In addition, what a privilege and honor to be invited by God to join Him in His great work of love as we help guide people away from Satan's deceptions and hurtful ways into God's marvelous loving presence and light.

Anyone who stays on life's wide self-centered road without God will miss all of the great opportunities that God has available for each person. But, if we listen to God and turn to Him, He will start transforming our nature immediately to be more and more like His. We will have the honor and privilege of following Jesus, the promised Messiah, the Son of the Most High, and of experiencing the joy of seeing lives transformed to do good now and forever.

The only way that Jesus' followers can experience the fulness of joy that Jesus experienced at the Cross–and still does as He leads His Church–is to ***step out in faith*** into the ongoing spiritual battles ***and join God in the greatest rescue mission of all eternity***. Out of a growing genuine love for others, Jesus' followers experience great godly joy by being part of God's eternal holy family and help rescue those whom they have come to learn to love. ***There is no greater joy than leading others to God and seeing them saved from the consequences of unholy living now and in the future with sin's ultimate disaster of eternal separation from God in shame and pain!***

As we begin to understand how precious we are to God, let us make sure that we are not being tossed about as the waves on a rough sea. All Christians should live out their lives remembering that God has brought them out of darkness into His marvelous light so that they see reality much clearer than those not listening to Him. Over time, they become better and better followers of Jesus as they learn to trust God more and more through there interactions with Him. Each should occasionally reevaluate his or her journey with God and the Universal Church in order to make sure that they are following God's Word and Jesus' leadership faithfully.

In addition, Jesus' followers should put aside all anxiousness that they may have and demonstrate the ***victory*** that is theirs as they follow Him. If they do this, our Heavenly Father will continually transform and empower them to be more and more like Jesus, which helps them become more and more effective as they work with God in His great work of love, which is the creation of His eternal close-knit holy family.

Through Jesus' leadership, we will provide a great witness and work! At various times under Jesus' leadership, we will unite and work in godly unity establishing strong individual, local church, community, and world-wide ministries. Accepting our Heavenly Father's love, righteousness, and sent son, Jesus, is the eternal solution to all problems. Whether we are doing normal daily work or something special, let's intentionally always strive to follow Jesus faithfully.

Now, as ***you*** finish this book, consider making a new or renewed commitment to God to open your heart more fully to His will for your life. If you have not done so already, commit to reading His Word on a regular basis, acting obediently to what you read, and faithfully following Jesus.

It is my personal prayer that reading this book has helped you obtain a closer walk with God. If I do not personally meet you on this side of eternity, I want you to know that it is my prayer that you have an exciting and rich life following our lord and savior Jesus the Christ, ***and let's all continually stay in a state of thanksgiving and celebration with Paul for the victory over death and sin that God has provided (1 Cor 15:50-58)!***

Appendix: Reading God's Word Accurately

It is important that ***all*** of Jesus' followers remain in God's inspired authoritative Word, the Bible, reading and living it out.[254] If they do not, Satan will slowly but surely recondition their minds toward accepting His deceptive lies.[255] Knowing that Jesus wants all of His followers to become more and more like Him should bring His followers to the place of reading our Heavenly Father's written Word on a regular basis and being in touch at all times with Him through ongoing open ended prayer. Prayer should normally be a two way street listening as well as speaking to God (2 Thess 5:17). ***Staying in God's Word, praying without ceasing, and keeping an open, obedient mind to God's leading is important for the highest level of success for Jesus' followers.***

It is important when studying God's Word not to misread it by forcing it to say something other than what it meant when it was originally written to its original recipients. If we understand what it originally meant, then we will be able to apply it to our present circumstances correctly.

There are some who incorrectly try to take what they are reading and consciously or subconsciously make it conform to what they have been taught by others or what they prefer it to mean. It is critical for all who want to understand God's Word accurately to allow God to teach them *what He actually is saying* through those who wrote under His inspiration. ***It is a common mistake to read into God's Word what we want it to say.***

If possible, keep in mind the literary and historical context along with grammar as you read through passages of the Bible and remember that all of the Bible fits together without contradictions.

---

[254] John 8:31b-32; Rom 12:1-2.

[255] John 8:43-44; 2 Cor 11:13-15.

So let's strive to understand it correctly knowing that all of the various scriptures work together well.

As you study God's Word, you may wish to have one or two good literal translations such as an English Standard Version (ESV) and/or a New American Standard Bible (NASB) along with one linguistically reconstructed translation (functional equivalent) such as the NIV, which rephrases the original text into wording that is more commonly understood today. The Living translations, sometimes called paraphrased translations, are useful for gaining *overall* perspective, but they are not good for in-depth understanding due to their loss of detail from God's original wording. Keep in mind that the Holy Spirit wants to be your guide to help you properly understand God and His Creation as you read the translations of your choice and seek truth.[256]

In addition to using a couple good translations, there are many good biblical study aids available such as Bible dictionaries, concordances, and commentaries that are very helpful in understanding the historical, cultural, and religious context while giving information that was common during ancient biblical times that span several thousand years.

But, always keep in mind that study aids including commentaries are not God's Word, and therefore be careful not to trust any of them as totally factual. There are other books that have been written to help individuals understand the various literary forms (genres) along with historical and literary contextual fundamentals. Keep in mind that even the most helpful books normally contain some bias that distorts parts of Scripture. Always ask God to guide your understanding as you read. If we listen to God, He will help us know truth (1 John 2:27). A major part of Jesus' mission was to help us understand what is real and what is not; He is the living Word of God (John 1:1-5, 14; 18:37; cf. 8:31b-32).

At all times, continue to pray and read God's Word, the Bible, living out what God teaches you. God speaks mightily to each of His children through His written Word and the continual leading of Jesus through the Holy Spirit, who helps us to

---

[256] 1 John 2:27; cf. 2 Tim 3:16-17; John 8:31b-32.

understand reality and the Father's desire for each of our lives (Heb 4:12). If you have not done so yet, join a local church and a Bible study group, listen to your minister(s), actively work within your church as led by the Spirit, and most importantly, ***do what God tells you through His Word and direct leading.*** Many fail to grow in their walk with God simply because they do not step out in faith and act on His leading (Heb 5:14).

References

Primary Sources

Biblia Hebraica Stuttgartensia. 3rd ed. Stuttgart: Deutsche Bibelgesellschaft, 1987.

The Greek New Testament. 3rd UBS ed. Stuttgart: Biblia-Druck, 1988.

General References

Bauer, Walter. *A Greek-English Lexicon of the New Testament and Other Early Christian Literature.* 5th ed. Translated and adapted by William F. Arndt & F. Wilbur Gingrich from the 4th rev. & augmented ed. of Walter Bauer's *Griechisch-Deutsches Wörterbuch zu den Schriften des Neuen Testaments und der übrigen urchristlichen Literatur*, 1958. Reprint: Chicago & London: The University of Chicago Press, 1979.

Blass, F. and DeBrunner A. *A Greek Grammer of The New Testament and Other Early Christian Literature.* Transl. and rev. from the 10th German ed. incorporating suppl. notes of A. Debrunner by Robert W. Funk. Chicago: London: Univ of Chicago Press; Cambridge Univ Press, 1961.

Blackaby, Henry. *Experiencing God.* Rev. ed. Nashville: Broadman and Holman, 2008.

Bonhoeffer, Dietrich. *Letters & Papers from Prison.* Rev. ed., ed. Eberhard Bethge. New York: Simon & Schuster, 1997.

Brown, Francis; Driver, S.R.; Briggs, Charles A. *The New Brown-Driver-Briggs-Gesenius Hebrew-English Lexicon.* Peabody, Mass: Hendrickson Publishers, 1979.

Corts, C. Mark. *The Truth about Spiritual Warfare: Your Place in the Battle Between God and Satan.* Nashville: Broadman & Holman, 2006.

Dodd, C. H. *The Interpretation of the Fourth Gospel.* New York: Cambridge University Press, 1953. Reprint: 1958.

Graham, Billy. *How To Be Born Again.* Waco: Word Books, 1977.

________. *The Journey: How To Live by Faith in an Uncertain World.* Nashville: W Publishing, 2006.

Hybels, Bill. *Just Walk Across the Room: Simple Steps Pointing People to Faith.* Grand Rapids: Zondervan, 2006.

Hybels, Bill and Mark Mittleburg, *Becoming a Contagious Christian*. Grand Rapids: Zondervan, 1994.

Innes, Dick. *I Hate Witnessing: A Handbook for Effective Christian Communications.* Rev. ed. San Clemente: Acts Communications, 2003.

Joseph, James B. *Experiencing Jesus' Joy*. Lynchburg, VA: Liberty University Press, 2013.

_______. *No More Walls! Creation of One New Man in Christ: Ephesians 2:11-22.* Saarbrücken: LAMBERT Academic Publishing, 2015.

_______. *The Ultimate Victory: Becoming a Follower of Jesus.* Pfafftown: IJSP, 2024.

Joseph, James B. *Unity and Obedient Discipleship in the Gospel of John.* 2nd ed. Pfafftown: IJSP, 2024.

Liddell, Henry George and Scott, Robert. *A Greek-English Lexicon.* Reprint of 9th ed., 1940. Revised and augmented by Henry Stuart Jones and Roderick McKenzie. London, New York & Toronto; Oxford University Press, 1990.

McDowell, Josh. *A Ready Defense.* San Bernardino: Here's Life, 1990, reprint 1991.

Metzger, Bruce M. *A Textual Commentary on the Greek New Testament.* Cor. ed. Germany: Biblia-Druck GmbH Stuttgart, 1975.

________. *The Text of The New Testament.* Oxford & New York: Oxford University Press, 1968.

Robertson, A.T. *A Greek Grammar of The New Testament: In Light of Historical Research.* 3rd ed. New York: Hodder & Stoughton, 1919.

Scouteris, Constantine. "The People of God-Its Unity and Its Glory: A Discussion of John 17:17-24 in the Light of Patristic Thought," *The Greek Orthodox Theological Review* 30, no. 4 (Winter 1985): 399-414.

Viehman, M.D., Greg E. *The God Diagnosis: a Physician's Shocking Journey to Life after Death.* Sylacauga, AL: Big Mac Publishers, 2010.

www.ingramcontent.com/pod-product-compliance
Lightning Source LLC
LaVergne TN
LVHW010916110826
845149LV00013B/2385
9798990596368